SAMSUNG S24 Ultra 5G Beginners and Seniors Guide

A Comprehensive user manual with tips and tricks to master the latest smartphone

Richard Isemonjie

Table of Contents

Chapter One: A Glance Through

Prepare your device

You may use nano-SIM cards with your device. Either a SIM card is already installed or you may use your existing one. The details and availability of your expert co-op's 5G organization are currently uncertain. To learn more about these nuances, consult your specialized co-op.

Charge your device
Before turning on your device, charge it fully.

Install SIM
Place the SIM card into the tray with the gold contacts facing up.

Just so you know, your device can withstand water and residue thanks to its IP68 classification. Make sure the SIM card plate apertures are dry and free of debris, and make sure the plate is firmly placed before exposing your device to fluids, to keep it water-and residue-safe.

Maintaining a barrier against water and residue

Warning: Avoid damaging your device or being shocked by charging it while damp or in a damp environment. Try not to interact with the device, charger, or cables with moist hands while it is charging.

Water and residue might ruin the device in any scenario. It is vital for guaranteeing every compartment is closed tightly.

Cautiously follow to these instructions to shield the device from injury and keep up with its protection against residue and water:

- The IP68 rating, which assesses submersion in freshwater for longer than 30 minutes or more profound than 1.5 meters, determines water opposition. To avoid fluid from entering the framework, each device that has accessible compartments or ports that may be opened need to have them fixed or sealed securely. If the item comes into touch with fresh water, totally dry it with a spotless, delicate material; if it comes into contact with any other form of fluid, flush it under new water and dry it as coordinated.

- Sound quality during a call might be impaired on the off chance that the gadget has been wet or on the other hand on the off chance that the receiver or speaker are sodden. Ensure the device is fully dry prior to employing it by washing it down with a dry rag. Avoid lowering the device under strong water stress. Whenever dropped or damaged by anything, the gadget's water and residue obstruction highlights can be harmed. On the off chance that residue or other articles get into the amplifier, speaker, or benefactor, the gadget can cease operating or its sound might change out to be peaceful. Endeavoring to erase the residue or various things with a sharp tool might injure the device and ruin its look.
- The air vent opening can become noisy when settling on telephone choices or playing media if a frill of any type covers it.

Significant NOTE: Different fluids could enter the device faster than pure water. The gadget can confront practical or fashionable difficulties in the event that it isn't entirely cleansed with fresh water and dried as per the instructions.

Recharge the battery

Your gadget's battery can be recharged.

Take note of the accessibility of a separate wall charger. Use only Samsung-supported chargers and ropes. To safeguard yourself and your device, never use faulty, damaged, or inconsistent batteries, chargers, or ropes. Changing out the batteries and charging hardware may damage the item and invalidate the warranty. For more information about your device, including charging compatibility, please visit samsung.com.

Guidance: During the charging process, the device and charger may overheat. This is usually within the device's normal operating range and has no effect on its life or performance. Allow the device to cool before removing the charger.

Wireless Power Sharing

Any feasible Samsung device may be remotely charged using your phone. Despite the fact that power is shared, certain parts remain inaccessible.

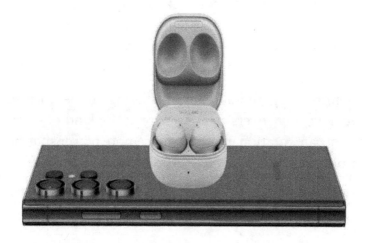

1. In the Settings menu, choose ⊚ Battery and device support > Battery > Remote power sharing.

2. After choosing a pace, choose "Battery limit." When the device you're charging reaches this point in control, remote power sharing turns off.

3. Press ⚪ to start the charging mechanism.

4. With the phone overcoming, place the viable device on the back of the phone to begin charging. When charging begins, you may feel a sensation or hear a sound.

☼ **NOTE**: Most Qi-Affirmed devices are compatible with remote power sharing. Must share at least 30% of the battery. Each contraption has a unique power production and charging rate. The maker's coverings, connectors, and other devices may not function as planned. If you're having trouble connecting or believe charging is taking up the most of your day, remove the covers from each device.

Before using remote power sharing, remember to remove any covers or connectors. The kind of cover or ornamentation may prevent remote power sharing from operating properly.

• Move your device to establish an association since each may have a different remote charging loop area.

When an association is set up, you will sense a vibration or notice that charging has commenced.

• Charging speed and productivity may vary depending on device condition and weather. Call collection and information services may also be affected depending on the organization's situation.

• Avoid utilizing earbuds when complaining of remote power sharing.

Put your device to work.

Turn on the device.

To turn on your mobile phone, press the Side key. Try not to use the device if its body is damaged or broken. After the device has been repaired, just use it.

○ To turn on the device, press and hold the Side key.

• To turn off the device, press and hold the Side and Volume down buttons simultaneously. Then choose "Power off". Confirm when addressed.

• To restart your device, press and hold the Side and Volume Down buttons simultaneously. Then, at that point, choose Restart. Confirm when addressed.

Guidance: To learn how to turn off your device, go to Settings > High level elements > Side key > How to shut off your phone.

NOTE: For optimal 5G performance, there should be no obstructions between the receiving wires on the back of the device. Contact your specialized co-op to find out which groups are open. A case or cover may impact 5G execution.

Utilize the Design Wizard.

When you first power on your device, the Arrangement Wizard walks you through the basic setup tasks.

To choose a default language, configure a Wi-Fi® network connection, create accounts, pick region administrations, locate your device's components, and that's only the tip of the iceberg, just follow the instructions.

Move data from an outmoded device

Download the Savvy SwitchTM app to transfer contacts, photos, music, videos, messages, notes, schedules, and more from your previous device using a PC, Wi-Fi, or USB connection.

1. From the Settings menu, choose 🔁 Records and reinforcement > Bring information from an old device.

2. Follow the steps to choose the material to move.

Turn off or open your device

Use the screen lock feature to keep your device safe. When the screen turns off, the device automatically locks.

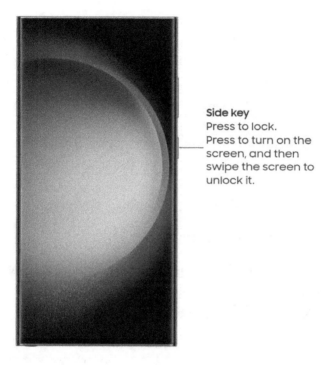

Side key
Press to lock.
Press to turn on the screen, and then swipe the screen to unlock it.

Accounts

Make and manage your records.

💡 **TIP:** Records can protect email, calendars, contacts, and other important information.

Create a Google Account.

Go to your Google Account to access introduced apps, Google Distributed storage, and the full potential of your phone's AndroidTM operating system.

Setting up a lock screen and connecting into your Google account are two steps in enabling Google Gadget Security. Your Google Record details are necessary to do an industrial facility reset.

1. In the Settings menu, choose 🔄 Records and reinforcement > Oversee accounts.

2. Under ➕ "Add account," choose Google.

Create a Samsung account.

Sign in to your Samsung account to fully use their apps and receive exclusive content. Choose Samsung account from the Settings menu.

Create a Viewpoint account.

Access your Outlook® account to see and manage email messages.

1. In the Settings menu, choose 🔄 Records and reinforcement > Oversee accounts.

2. Under ➕ Add account, choose Viewpoint.

Create a phone message.

You may configure your voice message administration when you sign in. Phone messages may be accessed using the Telephone program. Specialist organizations might introduce a range of choices.

1. You may choose Voice message from the Telephone menu **C** or press and hold the 1 key ⌐1⌐ .

2. Enter your secret word, hello, and name using the instructions provided.

Exploring

For light addresses, touch screens, a finger cushion, or a capacitive pointer are the best options. If the touch screen is pressed excessively hard or with a metallic object, it may be damaged; this kind of damage is not covered by warranty.

Apply pressure.

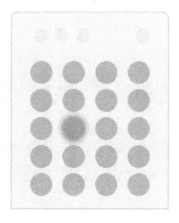

To choose or send out an item, gently touch it.

• Tap an object to choose it.

• To zoom in or out of a photo, double-tap it.

Take a swipe

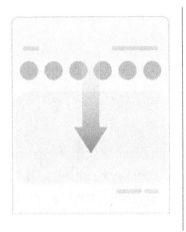

Use your finger to touch and move the screen gently.

• To open the gadget, swipe the screen.

• Swipe to navigate between Home screens and menu items.

Proceed to drop

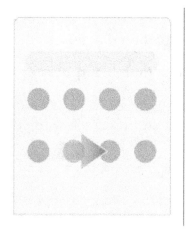

• Move an object to another location after receiving and contacting it.

• Alternately drag an application to your Home screen.

To transfer a device, simplify it.

Zoom in/out

To zoom in or out, move your thumb and fingers closer together or further apart on the screen.

• To magnify, separate your thumb and pointer on screen.

• To zoom out, press and hold the screen with your thumb and fingers.

Feel and take hold of

Contact and hold an object to make it move.

• Holding down on a field displays a pop-up menu of options.

•Touch and hold a Home screen to personalize it.

The menu bar

To navigate your phone, use the route keys or full screen signals.

Recent apps ——— III ○ < ——— Back

Navigation buttons

Use the buttons at the bottom of the screen to quickly explore.

1. In the Settings menu, choose Show > Route bar > Buttons.

2. Under Button request, choose which side of the screen displays the Back and Ongoing application icons.

Navigation gestures

Conceal the route buttons at the bottom half of the screen to free up the whole area. Overall, use a swipe to navigate your device.

1. To activate the element, go to Settings > Show > Route bar > Swipe signals.

2. Choose an option to redo:

• Additional options: Select the signal kind and response.

• Here's a clue: Use the lines in the bottom section of the screen to indicate where each screen motion is located.

Switch between apps when the clue is hidden: However, even when the motion suggestion is turned off, you may still use it to navigate between programs. Empowering this choice is critical.

• Display the console hiding button: To hide the console while the device is in representation mode, display the symbol in the bottom right corner of the screen.

• S Pen block movements are restricted to the WorldS24 Ultra.

Redesign the look of your home screen.

The Home screen on your device is where you begin your path. You may customize your favorite apps and gadgets here, as well as add new Home screens, remove screens, move screens, and choose a certain Home screen.

Symbols for applications

You may use an application's emblem to launch it from any Home screen.

○ From the Applications menu, click and hold an application icon, then choose ⊕ Add to Home.

○ Contact and hold an application icon on the Home screen, then choose 🗑 Eliminate to remove it.

☀ Note: When a symbol is removed, the program is not erased; it is only removed from the Home screen.

Background picture

You may quickly alter the Home and Lock screens by selecting the default background or your favorite image or video.

1. From the Home screen, tap and hold the screen to choose 🖼 background and style.

2. Tap one of the options below to see the different backdrops:

• Tap the images to change the Lock screen and Home screen backgrounds.

• Change the background: Choose from a variety of backdrop options, or purchase more ones from Universe Subject.

• Variety plot: Choose a strategy based on the tones in your background.

• Faint background while utilizing the Dim mode: Allow the Dull mode to be used on your backdrop.

Select a subject for your home and lock screens, foundations, and app symbols.

1. From the Home screen, touch and hold the screen.

2. To see and download a topic, just touch on it

3. Select Menu > My Things > Subjects to see the downloaded subjects.

4. Choose a subject, then click Apply to apply it.

Symbols Adding

Additional symbol sets allows you to modify implicit symbols.

1. From the Home screen, touch and hold the screen.

2. To view and download a symbol set, go to Subjects > Symbols and click on it.

3. Go to Menu > My Things > Symbols to see the downloaded symbols.

4. After selecting a symbol, tap Apply to apply the chosen symbol set.

Add widgets to your home screen for quick access to information or apps.

1. From the Home screen, touch and hold the screen.

2. Go to ⚪⚪ Widgets and choose a gadget to access a variety of gadgets.

3. To add a gadget to your home screen, slide over it and tap Add.

Modify gadgets.

After adding a device, you may modify its location and functionality.

○ From the Home screen, contact and hold a device, then press one of the following:

⊞ • Create a stack: Place other devices on the screen in a similar location by stacking them on top of one another.

🗑 • Eliminate: Take a device off your screen.

⚙ • Settings: Change the look or functionality of ⓘ the device.

• Application details: Examine the device's use, permissions, and other details.

arrangements for the major screen.

Re-do the home and application displays.

1. From the Home screen, touch and hold the screen.

2. To change, choose ⚙ Settings:

   • Home screen design: Configure your phone to have distinct displays for Home and Applications, or to have a single Home screen that includes all of your applications.

   • Lattice for the home screen: Select a pattern to represent how the symbols are structured.

   • Applications screen framework: Select a design to address the symbol location on the Applications screen.

   • Envelope lattice: Select a design to determine the organizer's structure.

   • Add a media page to the home screen. When enabled, swipe right from the home screen to access the media page. To see the available media administrations, touch.

   • Show the Applications screen button on the home screen: Remember to include a button on the Home screen that allows for easy access to the Applications screen.

• Lock the Home screen's course of action to prevent unauthorized users from changing or deleting items.

• Add new apps to the home screen: When an app is downloaded that seems interesting, it is automatically added.

• Protect apps on the Home and Application screens. Select an application to remove it from the Home and Application screens. Return to this screen to restore stowed apps. It is suitable for buried apps that have not yet been launched to appear in the Locator look.

• Enable identifications to appear on application symbols for applications that are currently receiving warnings. Another choice is the identification strategy.

• Swipe down to reveal warning board: When enabled, you may access the Notice board by swiping down from any location on the Home screen.

• Pivot to scene mode: When your device switches from image to scene mode, the Home screen rotates accordingly.

• The About screen allows you to examine form details.

• Talk to us: Contact Samsung support via Samsung Individuals.

Fundamental mode.

With the Simple mode design, the visual experience is simplified by using larger text and symbols. Instead of the default screen design, choose a less challenging configuration.

Display> Easy mode.

1. Select Settings, then ⚙️ Display > Easy Mode.

2. Tap ⬤ to make this feature dynamic. The following options become noticeable:

• Contact and hold delay: Determine how long it takes for a consistent contact to initiate a touch and hold.

• High differentiation console: Choose a console with clearly separated colors.

Status signal

Gadget data appears on the right side of the Status bar, whereas notice warnings appear on the left.

Status Symbols

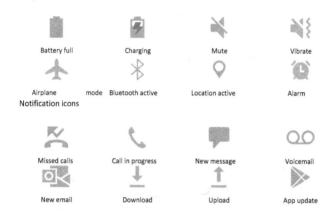

Set the status bar's showcase options.

Guidance: To personalize the status bar notices, go to the Speedy Settings menu and choose More options > Status Bar.

Notice board

To rapidly access settings, notifications, and other highlights, just visit the Notice board.

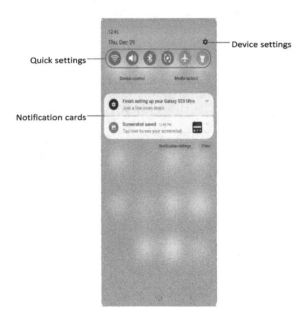

Quick settings

Device settings

Notification cards

Check the Notification Board.

The Warning board may be seen on any screen.

1. When you slide down on the screen, you will see the Warning Board.

    • To open anything, tap it.

    • To remove a single caution, drag the notice to the left or right.

    • To remove all warnings, hit Clear.

    • To change notices, choose Notice settings.

2. To shut the Warning board, choose ⟨ Back or drag it up from the bottom of the screen.

Fast settings.

The Warning board provides quick access to device capabilities via Speedy settings. The icons below represent the most well-known Fast settings. A symbol's diversity fluctuates depending on whether it is empowered or disabled. There could be additional options available on your device.

1. Drag the Status bar down to see the Warning board.

2. Swipe down from the top of the screen again to see the Fast Settings.

• Use the fast settings icon to switch it on/off.

• Press and hold the icon to get a quick setting. Whereabouts, energy conservation, dim mode, Bluetooth, Wi-Fi, and auto revolution are all incorporated.

| Wi-Fi | Sound | Bluetooth | Auto rotate |

| Airplane mode | Location | Power saving | Dark mode |

Quick settings options

The following options are available in Speedy Settings.

• Locator: Investigate the device.

• Power off: Choose between restarting and turning off the PC.

• Settings: Easily navigate the gadget's settings menu.

• More options: change the request for the buttons or alter the Fast settings.

• Gadget Control: If you have suitable programs installed, like as Google Home or SmartThings, you may use them to control other devices.

• Media yield: Navigate to the Media board to manage the playing of compatible audio and video devices.

• Splendor slider: Drag to adjust the screen's brightness.

S Pen

The S Pen offers numerous useful features. Use your S Pen to access programs, take notes, and draw diagrams. Certain S Pen features, such as touchscreen tapping (notably on the UniverseS24

Ultra), may not operate if the phone is adjacent to a magnet.

S Pen button

Draw out the S pen

The S Pen is stored in the bottom section of your device for easy access. The S Pen should also be charged before using it for remote capabilities.

○ To deliver the S Pen, push it within and then slide it out.

Note: To maintain the device's water- and residue-resistant features, keep the S Pen area and opening dry and free of flotsam and jetsam, and ensure the pen is securely positioned before exposing it to fluids.

View from a higher spot

Move the S Pen over an object on the screen to reveal additional information or to view it. In air view, you may access to the following highlights:

• Check an email before opening it.

• Explore a picture gallery or expand an image.

• Easily get to a certain scene and examine a video by scrolling across the timeline.

• Look up the name or image of a sign or button.

Perception: Only when the see option is enabled will the S Pen's on-screen pointer be clearly colored.

Air moves

The S Pen may be used to do workouts from a distance by pressing the button and completing certain movements or developments. You can do errands, swipe between shows on your devices, provide quick access to the programs you use most often, and much more.

The S Pen remote element is only compatible with Bluetooth Low Energy (BLE) pens that have received Samsung certification. The S Pen disconnects from the device if it is too far away or if there is a barrier. The S Pen must be linked for air operations to take place.

To enable the component, go to the Settings menu and choose Progressed Highlights > S Pen > Air Activities.

Press the other way key to activate the S Pen button.

Holding down the S Pen button allows you to create an easy path. Naturally, this option sends the Camera application.

1. Choose High level elements > S Pen > Air workouts from the Settings menu.

2. To activate the element, hold down the Pen button and tap .

Actions performed wherever.

Anyplace activities are programmable alternative methods that may be accessed by holding the S Pen button while doing one of the following motions: up, down, left, right, or shaking. Open from each screen, they include apps, S Pen highlights, and routes.

Action	Gesture

Back	Left to right
Recents	Right to left
Home	Up and down
Smart select	Down and up
Screen write	Zigzag

1. Choose ⊕ High level elements > S Pen > Air workouts from the Settings menu.

2. To modify the simple way, tap the Signal sign under Anyplace Activities.

Application-driven exercises

You may use your S Pen to complete special activities in select apps.

1. Choose ⊕ High level elements > S Pen > Air workouts from the Settings menu.

2. Tap an application to see the accessible, simple ways.

3. Tap to use the simple routes while using that app.

Normal activities of an application

You may change a few frequent tasks when using camera and media apps that are not mentioned in the application activity list.

1. Choose High level elements > S Pen > Air workouts from the Settings menu.

2. To modify a movement, tap it under Broad application workouts.

Turn off the reminder.

You may create reminders when the screen is turned off. The screen off notification option should be enabled.

1. When the screen is off, take out the S Pen and write anything on it.

2. Select one of the following to tailor your update:

• Variety: Vary the pen's tone.

• Tap to utilize the pen gadget. Tap again to adjust the line thickness.

• Use the eraser by pushing it. Tap again to remove everything.

3. Tap store to store your reminder in the Samsung Notes app.

NOTE If you have already removed the S Pen from the device, press the S Pen button and touch the screen to start a note when the screen is turned off.

Hold it generally in your squeeze.

A note in Consistently In Plain View may be updated or stuck.

1. Contacting Pin allows you to choose between Consistently In Plain View and Screen-Off notice.

2. Actuate the Consistently In Plain View highlight.

Air Instructions:

Use any screen to access the various S Pen features, such as Samsung Notes, Brilliant Select, and Screen Compose.

Settings

1. To activate the pointer, hold the ⬤ S Pen near to the screen or press the Air order. At that moment, hit the S Pen button once.

2. Choose a choice.

• Start another note: Close the Samsung Notes program and start another note.

• View each note: Launch the Samsung Notes app to view a list of the many notes you've created.

- Brilliant selection: Draw a circle around a portion of the screen to collect it for the display.

app.

- Screen compose: Include text or representations in your screen shots.

- Live messages: Using the S Pen, compose or draw a quick, animated message.

- AR Doodle: Use the included AR camera to create intuitive doodles.

- Decipher: Hover the S Pen pointer over a word to see its translation into another dialect and hear it spoken.

- PENUP: Use the S Pen to create, vary, edit, and share live drawings.

- Add: Expand the Air order menu's list of applications and functionality.

- Settings: To recreate an Air order, adjust the way the Air order menu rotates and move the apps and highlights up.

Take notice.

Open the Samsung Notes app and start writing a new note right now.

Click ⬤ Air Order > ⊕ Make Notes.

 Analyze each note.

◦ Open the Samsung Notes application to view a ⬇ list of the notes you've created.

To display all notes, choose ⬤ Air Order and then ⬙ View All Notes.

A smart option.

The Savvy Select feature allows you to replicate content from any screen. Following that, you might include it in your Exhibition application or share it with your acquaintances.

1. Hold down ⬤ Air Order and choose ⬙ Smart Select.

2. Drag the S Pen over a shape from the menu to choose content. The following options become apparent:

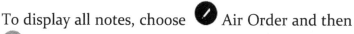 • Pin/Supplement: You may either directly integrate the collected content into an application or put a quick link to it on your home screen.

• Auto select: Allow Brilliant Select to choose material for extraction on its own.

• Draw: Use the recorded content to create outlines.

• Extricate text: Locate and remove text from the chosen source.

• Share: To share your content, choose a sharing option.

3. Tap Save should be selected.

Guidance: Press ⌜GIF⌝ Movement to start recording liveliness. Click ⌜📌⌝ Pin to Screen to utilize Shrewd Select to add stuff to your screen.

Put text to the screen.

Screen write allows you to explain or draw on screen captures.

1. On the compose screen, choose ◉ Air Order > Compose.

2. Catching the dynamic screen brings up a pen instrument. The following modifying apparatuses are open:

• Crop: Drag the screen's edges to resize the captured content.

• Pen type: Sketch using the screen capture. Tap the Pen picture again to adjust the pen tip, size, and variety.

 • Eraser: Remove all text and images from the screen shot.

• Fix: Reverse the prior move.

 • Retry: Rehash the previous action that was dispersed.

 • Share: To share your content, choose a sharing option.

• Scroll catch: Take a snapshot of any area of the screen that may be overlooked or covered up.

3. Tap Save should be selected. The material is protected in the Display application.

Hold down the S Pen button to remove your doodles from the screen reminder.

Texting

Record a lively drawing or a written message.

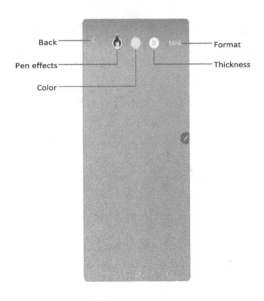

Back — Format

Pen effects — Thickness

Color

1. Select ♡ Live Messages from the ⊘ Air Command Menu.

2. Select a foundation from the following options:

• View your Assortment messages in real-time.

• Select an image or video to use as the basis.

• Take a photo for the foundation.

• Choose a variation for your foundation.

3. Follow the steps to begin creating your live message.

4. Click Done to save.

AR Doodle

Use extended reality to create intelligent drawings on people and other things visible to the camera.

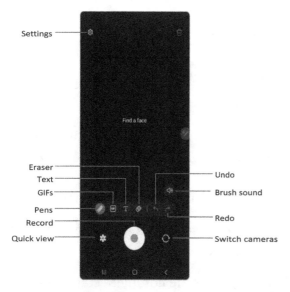

1. Select ⬡ AR Doodle from the ⬤ Air Order menu.

2. To switch between the front and rear cameras, choose Switch ⬤ cameras.

3. Position the camera such that your aim is the primary focus of the photograph.

4. Create a doodle with the S Pen.

• The doodle continually tracks the growth of the face.

5. Tap ● Record to capture a video of your AR Doodle.

The images you see here are just meant to be used as a point of reference since programming and equipment are constantly evolving.

Decipher

Drift your mouse over words to hear their pronunciation and decipher them with the S Pen.

1. To decode, press ●Air order > ⒶInterpret.

2. Tap the icon to choose between decoding a word and interpreting an expression.

• Phrases: Make sense of the complete statement.

• Words: Interpret a word.

3. Tap them to switch the source and destination dialects to the desired dialects.

4. Place the pointer of the S Pen over an expression.

• Tap 🔊 Sound to hear the word spoken in its native language.

• Tap 🗐 Duplicate to store the selected text and its interpretation to your clipboard.

5. Tap ✕ near the escape Decipher.

PENUP

Use the S Pen to create, vary, change, and share drawings on a continual basis.

- Press or snap 🖊 Air Order > ♠ PENUP.

Consolidate other methods

You may redesign the Air order menu by providing alternative paths to other apps and features.

1. Select 🖊 Air order > ➕ Add First.

2. Tap on the apps or functionality you want to access from the Air order menu.

• To remove an application's simple route, choose ➖ Eliminate.

3. To save your option, click the ‹ route up button.

Designs for Air Order

An intuitive folding menu anywhere on the screen allows you to quickly access apps and S Pen highlights.

○ To modify the accompaniment, go to Settings > ⚙ Progressed Highlights > S Pen > Air Order.

• Customize how the Air order menu opens.

• Browse Air Order's easy routes.

• The Air order sign will appear in the menu.

• To access the Air order menu, use the Pen or S Pen buttons.

Design the S Pen's settings.

The S Pen has a variety of settings. Every expert organization makes distinctive judgments.

○ To alter the accompaniment, choose High level elements > S Pen from the Settings menu

• Settings: Air Activities: Customize the controller's functionality when using applications.

• Customize the Air order menu, including look, behavior, and other routes.

• Air view may be switched on/off.

• Use the S Pen to write in text fields, address bars, and other areas where text is visible. Using the S Pen, you may make modifications to the text that has been transferred from your handwriting.

• When the S Pen is removed, which of the following occurs? Decide whether to sit idle, make a note, or place an outside order.

• For screen off updates, disable the S Pen and scribble on the screen while composing a note. Off-screen notes are saved in Samsung Notes.

• To take fast notes, press and hold the S Pen button and touch the screen twice to start a new note.

• Customize S-Pen settings, including associations, vibrations, and suggestions.

• Inspect the specific features of the S Pen edition.

• To contact Samsung support, please utilize Samsung Individuals.

Bixby

Bixby, a menial worker, evolves and becomes more like you. It remembers your preferences, connects with your favorite apps, and helps you schedule updates based on the date, time, and location.

○ On the Home screen, press and hold the Side key.

The Applications section also provides access to Guidance Bixby.

Bixby Visual Help

Bixby has been integrated with your Web, Exhibition, and Camera programs to help you figure out what you're seeing. It provides context-based symbols for business, milestone recognition, QR code validation, and interpretation.

Camera

Bixby Vision is available in the camera viewfinder to help you interpret what you see.

○ Select Additional > Bixby Vision from Camera, then follow the directions.

Display

Photographs and images stored in the Display app are compatible with Bixby Vision.

1. To see a photograph in the Exhibition, contact it.

2. Press Bixby Vision and then the headers.

Web

When a picture appears in the Web application, you may utilize Bixby Vision to find out additional information about it.

1. Tap and hold a photo from the Web to see a pop-up menu.

2. Select Search with Bixby Vision, then follow the on-screen prompts.

Examples & Modes

Configure modes and schedules so that your device's settings vary in response to your workouts and location.

To customize the resultant pages, choose ⊙ Modes and Schedules from the Settings menu.

• Modes: Choose a mode based on what you are doing or where you are right now.

• Schedules: Make phone plans based on places or hours.

Computerized prosperity and parental control

You can detect and manage your digital tendencies by tracking your daily application usage, number of warnings, and frequency of device inspections. You may also program your device to help you relax before going to bed.

Navigate to Settings, ⊙ Advanced Prosperity, and Parental Controls to get the following highlights:

• Tap the Dashboard to see the following:

- Screen time: See how long an application is open and used each day.

- Caution: Check the number of alerts an application has sent you in a particular day.

- Times opened/Opened: View the recurring purpose of an application throughout the course of a day.

• Set a screen time goal and monitor the amount of time you spend on screens each day.

• Application clocks: Maintain a daily record of how long you spend on each application.

• Driving screen: Use your vehicle's Bluetooth to track which apps you use the most and how much time you spend on screens.

• Volume screen: Choose a sound source that allows you to screen the volume while protecting your hearing.

• Parental controls: Use Google's Family Connection app to monitor your children's online activities. You may establish screen time restrictions, apply content channels, and choose which apps to launch.

Continuously in plain view

Consistently in Plain View (AOD) allows you to see missed calls and messages without having to open your device, as well as the time and date and other customizable information.

1. From the Settings menu, choose 🔒 Lock screen > Consistently In Plain View.

2. After touching 🔘 to activate the usefulness, adjust the following boundaries:

• Choose when to enable alerts and a clock on your device while it's not in use.

• Clock style: You may alter the tone and layout of the clocks under Consistently under Plain View and Lock Screen.

• Show music subtleties: Use the FaceWidgets music regulator to display music subtleties.

• Screen direction: The AOD offers two modes: representation and scenario.

• Auto brilliance: You may vary the magnificence of the Consistently in plain sight naturally.

• In clear view: confirm the introduced programming form and permit data.

AOD topics

Tailor the topic of Consistently In Plain View.

1. Contact and hold the screen from the Home screen, then choose 🖌 Topics > AODs.

• Tap an AOD to evaluate and save it to My Generally On Showcases.

2. To see the downloaded topics, choose ☰ Menu > My Things > AODs.

3. Once an AOD has been selected, click Apply.

Biometric security.

Use biometrics to securely unlock your device and login in to your accounts.

Recognizing the face

To open your screen, enable face recognition software. To use your face to unlock your phone, first establish an example, PIN, or secret key.

•Face authentication is less secure than examples, PINs, and passwords. It might be any person or item that seems to be you that unlocks your device.

• Some face recognition challenges include beards, spectacles, coverings, and needless cosmetics.

• Before registering your face, make sure the camera's focus point is clean and you're in a well-lit environment.

1. From the Settings menu, choose ⬤ Security & Protection > Biometrics > Face Recognition.

2. Follow the bearings into your face.

Controlling facial acknowledgment

Change the face recognition framework's capabilities.

○ Go to Settings > ⬤ Security and Protection > Biometrics > Face Recognition.

• To dispose of facial information, wipe existing countenances.

• Provide an unmistakable look to enhance recognition: Improve face recognition by including a specific appearance.

• Face open: Use face recognition to activate or disable security.

• Keep the screen locked until you swipe: Stay on the Lock screen until you swipe the screen to unlock your device using face recognition.

• With your eyes open, facial recognition software may detect your face.

• Brighten the screen briefly to let you see your face in low-light conditions.

• Learn more about face acknowledgment and how to use it to unlock your phone.

Fingerprint scanner

Instead of typing passwords, use unique mark acknowledgment in specific programs.

You may also use your unique finger imprint to authenticate who you are while entering into your Samsung account. Before you can use your fingerprint to unlock your phone, you must first specify an example, PIN, or secret word.

1. From the Settings menu, choose 🔘Security & Protection > Biometrics > Fingerprint.

2. Follow the guidelines to register your distinctive mark.

Treatment of fingerprints

Rename, remove, and add fingerprints.

Navigate to ⬤ Security and Protection > Biometrics > Fingerprints in the Settings menu to access the relevant options.

• This list begins with a breakdown of enlisted fingerprints. Tapping on a finger imprint allows you to rename or delete it.

• Add a distinctive mark: Simply follow the directions to enroll a subsequent finger imprint.

• Look at the additional fingerprints: Output your unique finger imprint to see whether it was recorded.

Set up limits for distinct finger imprint confirmation.

Use unique mark acknowledgment in activities and initiatives that allow you to affirm your individuality.

To enable fingerprint authentication, go to the Settings menu and choose ⬤ Security and Protection > Biometrics.

• Unique finger impression open: Use your finger imprint to open your device and reveal your identity.

• Always on unique mark: Use your finger imprint to examine the screen even while it is off.

• Display the unique finger imprint sign when the screen is turned off.

• Display an action when opening: If you tick the distinctive mark box, a movement will display.

• As to: Learn more about how to safeguard your device using fingerprints.

Biometric courses of action.

Determine your preferences for biometric security highlights.

To enable biometrics, go to the ⬤ Security and Protection section in the Settings menu.

• Display an open change impact: When you open your device with your finger imprint, it will display a progress bar.

• Biometric opening: Learn more about using biometrics to unlock your device.

Multiple windows.

Multitasking is the act of using numerous apps at the same time. Because of split screen capabilities, applications that aid Multi WindowTM may be viewed alongside one another. You may navigate between projects and adjust the size of their windows.

Split screen control.

Working with a double screen

1. From any screen, choose ||| Late Applications.

2. To exit in split screen mode, press the program's icon.

3. Tap an application in the opposite window to add it to the split screen view.

Drag the middle of the line to alter the window size.

Window arrangements

Using the Window controls modifies how the split screen view program windows appear.

1. To modify the window size, drag the center of the window boundaries.

2. Tapping the focal point of the window line will provide the following options:

• Switch windows: Switch between the two windows.

• Consolidate application pair: Create an alternative application pair and add it to the edge screen's Applications Board.

Panels that surround the edges.

Edge boards, accessible from the screen's edge, provide a variety of configurable boards. Edge boards allow you to access errands, contacts, apps, and other information while also reviewing news, sports, and other content.

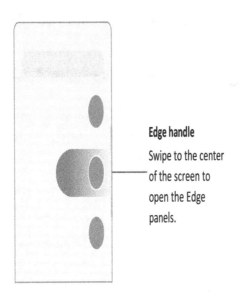

Edge handle

Swipe to the center of the screen to open the Edge panels.

Go to the Settings menu and choose ⚙ Show > Edge Boards, tap ⬤ to enable.

Panel of applications

It is possible to add apps to the apps area.

1. Drag the Edge handle to any screen's focus point. To see the Applications board, slide.

2. To open an application or an application pair, tap
••• its opposite method. On the other side, you may
tap All programs to see the whole list of applications.

• Open several windows in spring up view by
dragging the program icon from the Applications
menu to the open screen.

Introducing the Application Board:

1. Drag the Edge handle to any screen's focus point.
To see the Applications board, slide.

2. Tap ◢ Alter to add other programs to the
programs pane.

• To add an application to an accessible circumstance
on the right segment of the Applications board,
choose it from the left side of the screen and push the
button.

• Drag an application from the left half of the screen
onto an application in the right side to provide a
simple path for an organizer.

• Simplified all of the board's project requests.

• To uninstall a program, choose ▬ Remove.

3. Tap ❬ Back to save your changes.

Restructure the edge boards.

Edge boards have customizable parameters.

1. Selecting Boards from 🔆 Show > Edge boards > Settings

2. The options available to you are as follows:

✓ • Checkbox: Show regardless of whether each board is dynamic.

🔍 • Search: Locate boards that have been proactively launched or can be introduced.

• Alter: If possible, place each board separately.

• Different options:

- Reorder the boards by dragging them to the left or right.

- Uninstall: Remove any downloaded Edge boards from your device.

- Conceal on Lock screen: Select which boards to hide on the Lock screen when a solid screen lock is enabled.

• Galaxy Store: Use the Cosmic System Store to look for and download more Edge boards.

3. Tap ⟨ Back to save your changes.

Arrangement and style of edge board

The Edge handle is moveable.

To see the associated options, go to the Settings menu and choose ⚙ Show > Edge boards > Handle.

• Drag the ⌄ Edge handle to change its position on the screen's edge.

• Position: Use the Right or Passed on button to select which side of the Edge screen to display.

• Lock handle position: This component allows you to contact and stand firmly on the handle footing without moving.

• Style: Select the shade of the Edge handle.

• Straightforwardness: Use the slider to adjust the straightforwardness of the Edge handle.

• Size: Use the slider to adjust the Edge handle's dimensions.

• Width: Drag the slider to adjust the Edge handle's width.

• Shake upon contact: When the Edge handle comes into contact, it shudders.

Concerning edge boards.

You can see the introduced programming variant as well as the permit data for the Edge boards' functionality.

○ From the Settings menu, pick 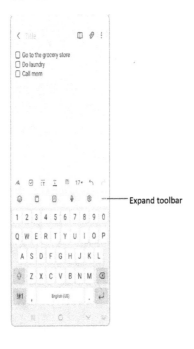 Show > Edge boards > About Edge boards.

Input words.

Text section is possible through discourse or a console.

Expand toolbar

Toolbar

The toolbar provides simple access to console functionality. Specialist organizations might introduce a range of choices.

○ In the Samsung console, select the Grow toolbar to view the following options:

• Articulation: Create custom blend emoticons, experiment with different emoticon types, and that's just the start.

• Clipboard: The clipboard can be found here.

• One-handed console: Switch to a console that can be operated with one hand.

• Voice input from Samsung should be used.

• Settings: View the console arrangement.

• Penmanship: (Cosmic System S24 Ultra only) Type text with your penmanship.

• Part console: Use a split console divided into equal parts.

• Drifting console: Replace the existing console with one that can be positioned anywhere on the screen.

• Search: Go through your previous collaborations and look for specific terms or expressions.

• Create an interpretation of: Use the console to type words or sentences in another dialect.

• Separate text: Locate the text in the chosen content and remove it.

• Samsung Pass: Use your fingerprints to quickly and securely access your data and web accounts.

• Grammarly: Grammarly suggests words to use while you type.

• Emoticons: Choose one to use here.

• GIFs: Also use animated GIFs.

• Bitmoji: Create your own custom emoji and use it on stickers.

• Mobitok: You can create your own stickers or use those that are naturally suggested.

• AR Emoticon: Create customized emoticons for use in stickers and for

• To add music, use SpotifyTM.

• YouTube: Use recordings from YouTube.

• Console aspects: Adjust the width and level of the console

• Content editing: Use an altering board to help you find the text to cut, duplicate, and glue.

Collect the Samsung console.

Change the settings on your Samsung console. Each specialist co-op makes decisions with remarkable determination.

○ In the Samsung console, click Settings to access the following settings:

• Dialects and types: Browse the available console dialects and select a console type. To switch between dialects, swipe the Space bar left or right.

Deft composing

• Prescient text: As you write, view suggested words and phrasing.

• Emoticon ideas: While utilizing prescient text, add emoticons.

• Prescribed stickers to glance at while composing: While you write, notice potential stickers.

• Auto supplant: This feature subsequently embeds advised content in place of your remark.

• Propose text amendments: Point out erroneous terms in red and provide ideas for changing them.

• Text simple routes: Make other approaches for most of the time employed phrases and sentences.

• More adaptable composing options: Give additional creating possibilities.

Course of action and style

• Console toolbar: Change whether it is visible or stored away.

• High difference console: You may modify the Samsung console's size and variety to strengthen the contrast between the keys and the foundation.

• Topic: Select a topic for your console.

• Mode: Pick between representation or scene formats.

• Size and Straightforwardness: Change the size and straightforwardness of the console.

• Design: Make use of the console to highlight remarkable characters and numerals.

• Text dimension: Utilize the slider to change the text dimension's.

• Custom pictures: You may alter the image's console simple ways.

Various game plans

• Voice input: Change the voice input administrations and settings.

• Swipe, contact, and criticism: The actions and input may be modified.

• Penmanship: Just available on the UniverseS24 Ultra, establish penmanship preferences.

• Messaging S Pen: Utilize the S Pen to write in address bars, search boxes, and other text fields. You can edit the text that has been changed over from your handwriting using the S Pen, which is simply possible with the WorldS24 Ultra.

• Permit the console to save screen grabs by authorizing it to save screen captures to the clipboard.

• Select whatever material from outsiders to utilize: Empower the outsider console options.

•Return to the initial arrangement: Remove the altered information from the first console setup.

About the Samsung console: View the adaptation and authentic facts about the Samsung console.

• Talk with us: To contact Samsung support, utilize Samsung Individuals.

Utilize the speech input on your Samsung device.

Rather of producing text, say it.

By choosing 🎤 Voice input on the Samsung console, you may direct your text.

Chapter Two: Camera and Gallery

Pictures and Exhibition

You may capture amazing images and videos employing the Camera program. Pictures and recordings placed aside in the Exhibition may be viewed and edited.

 **Camera Viewfinder**

Gain a wide assortment of master focal points despite high level video settings and modes. ○ Click on the Camera application.

Tip: Press the Side key two times fast to access the Camera application.

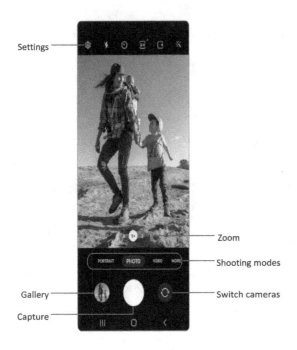

Settings

Zoom

Shooting modes

Switch cameras

Gallery

Capture

Explore the camera's screen.

Utilize your gadget's front and rear cameras to capture outstanding images.

1. In 📷 Camera, set up your shot using the appropriate boundaries:

• Tap the optimum region of the screen to focus the camera.

• Tapping on the screen allows a brilliance scale to flash up.

• Drag the slider to vary the brightness.

• To switch between the front and rear cameras, swipe up or down on the screen fast.

• Press 1x and thereafter a lower part of-the-screen selection to exactly zoom in. (Just available when employing the rear camera.)

• To shift to an alternative shooting mode, slide the screen right or left.

• To modify the camera settings, hit ⚙ Settings.

2. Use Tap to ⬭ capture a photo.

Design the way of shooting.

You may explore numerous different shooting modes, or you can trust the camera to determine the optimum setting for your images.

○ Swipe the screen both ways from the 📷 Camera to switch between shooting modes.

• Representation: Change the casing's experience to capture a picture photograph.

• Picture: Permit the camera to pick the optimal settings for images.

• Video: For optimum results, let the camera decide the settings.

• Extra: Browse a scope of shooting alternatives. To shift a mode in one direction or the other, push ⊕ Include the shooting modes plate at the bottom half of the camera screen.

- Master Crude: Download Master Crude to activate shooting mode.

- Star: Change the ISO awareness, white equilibrium, openness worth, and variation tone by hand when shooting images.

- Expert video: Utilize manual settings for ISO responsiveness, variation tone, openness worth, and white equilibrium when filming.

- In a solo shot: Take multiple images and videos from diverse locations.

- Scene: To give a straight image, snap photographs in either a flat or vertical bearing.

- Night: Utilize this to capture images in low light without using a blaze. - Food: Spotlight on capturing the beautiful hues of the food in your shots.

- Really slow movement: Recordings ought to be recorded at an exceptionally high edge rate to be noticed in spectacular sluggish movement. You have the opportunity to rapid forward or rewind sexual sections in a recorded video.

- Slow movement: Recordings taken shots at a high edge rate may be evident in slow movement.

- Hyperlapse: To produce a period pass movie, record at varying edge speeds. The edge rate is altered while contemplating the growth of the gadget and the scene being filmed.

- Picture video: Change the foundation of your photographs to fit the organization.

From the standpoint of the chief: Utilize current characteristics like latching onto a topic while it's in view, exchanging between rear camera focal points, and that's only the beginning.

AR Zone

You may get to the whole of your enhanced reality (AR) highlights from a single area.

○ Pick AR Zone by swiping to More from the Camera. The items recorded hereunder are open:

• AR Emoticon Studio: Make and personalize your My Emoticon symbol using AR equipment.

• AR Emoticon Camera: Utilize this gadget to construct your personal My Emoticon symbol.

• AR Emoticon Stickers: Apply AR stickers to personalize your My Emoticon symbol.

• AR Doodle: To better motion images, insert manually written comments or line drawings into your existing condition. With AR Doodle, you may track with by tracking their countenances and geographical places.

• Deco Pic: You can use the camera to add changes to images or recordings continually.

• Depiction: Utilize your camera to assess items in centimeters or inches.

Space Amplification

Catch images at up to multiple times amplification with clearness and exactness (WorldS24 Ultra as it were).

1. To pick the amplification level, press the Zoom other method from the Camera menu.

• Focus your goal in the edge and hit Zoom lock to guarantee rapid and perfect zoom centering when taking images at greater amplifications.

2. Use to snap a photo.

Make video accounts.

Make great, smooth recordings employing your telephone.

1. To shift to video mode, swipe right or left from the ⚫ camera.

2. To start recording a video, choose ● Record.

• To take a snapshot while the video is recording, 🔲 press Capture.

• To momentarily halt recording, press ‖ Delay. To keep recording, proceed with ■ .

3. Press Stop to terminate the recording.

360-degree capture of sound

Use your Bluetooth earbuds (independently available) to capture realistic 3D sound with 360 sound recording.

1. From the menu, search for the ⚫ camera, choose ⚙ Settings.

2. To commence 360 sound recording, pick 360 video choices.

Camera arrangements

Utilize the settings menu and major screen icons to modify the settings on your camera. Each expert co-op has an interesting determination of choices.

○ To view the following options, click ⚙ Settings from the 📷 Camera menu:

Clever highlights

• Scene analyzer: This feature subsequently modifies the various settings of your images to more easily fit the general atmosphere.

• Shot proposals: To aid you with making stunning photographs, follow the on-screen directions.

• Check QR codes: Utilize the camera to apprehend QR codes subsequently.

Pictures

• Swipe Screen button: You may choose to snap a burst image or generate a GIF by swiping the shade to the nearest edge.

• Watermark: Add a watermark to the bottom left corner of your images.

• Further improved image choices: Browse an array of record organizations and save options.

- High-proficiency photos: conserve photographs as high-effectiveness pictures to conserve space. It's feasible that few out of every unusual sharing site supports the setting.

- Ace mode picture design: To save your images, pick the Expert mode picture design.

Selfies

• Protect selfies in their review state: Don't rotate self-representations. All things considered, maintain them as they were.

Recordings

• Auto FPS: You could snap more dazzling low-light motion pictures by having Video mode consequently modify the edge rate.

• Video adjustment: When the camera is moving, set on enemy of shaking to keep a continuous attention.

• High level video choices: Utilize state of the art recording arrangements to boost your accounts.

- High-effectiveness recordings: Utilize the HEVC design when recording recordings to conserve capacity. Conceivable sharing sites or different devices won't support this arrangement's playback.

- High bitrate recordings (Genius video): To capture recordings in a greater piece rate, apply the Master video shooting option.

- HDR10+ recordings: To take use of your records, record in HDR10+. Playback equipment required to assist HDR10+ video.

- Zoom-in receiver: Ensure the camera and amplifier have identical zoom when capturing recordings.

- 360 sound recording: Utilize your Bluetooth earbuds to capture rich, three-layered sound.

In light of everything

• Following auto-center: Focus your concentration on a moving goal.

• Lattice lines: To aid in outlining a picture or video, display the matrix lines in the viewfinder.

• Area labels: Incorporate a GPS area label in your photographs and recordings.

• Shooting strategies: - Press the Volume keys to: Take photographs, make recordings, broaden, or modify the framework volume.

- Voice guidelines: Record yourself applying essential phrases.

- A drifting shade button is an extra screen button that may be moved about the screen.

- Show palm: Hold out your hand and face the camera to get your preview taken swiftly.

• Safeguarded settings: Pick whether to send off the camera in the previous visual mode, selfie point, and channels.

• Shade sound: Press a note when you capture a shot.

• Vibration criticism: You may begin vibrations when you push the screen by employing the Camera program.

Privacy

• Security Disclosure: Look at Samsung's protection guidelines.

• Permissions: Audit the needed and discretionary consents for the Camera application.

Others

• Configuration reset: Reset the layout of the camera. Contact us: To contact Samsung support, utilize Samsung Individuals.

• With regards to Camera: Access insights into programming and applications.

✳ Gallery

Go to the Exhibition on your smart phone to watch all of the put away video stuff. It is doable to watch, edit, and monitor photographs and videos.

○ Select ✳ Gallery by touching on Applications.

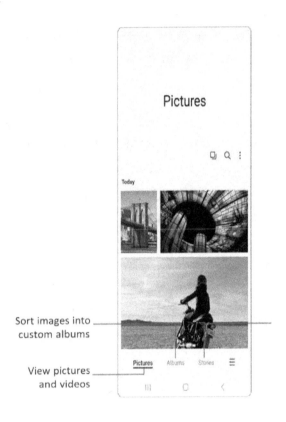

Sort images into
custom albums

View pictures
and videos

Check pictures out

The Display program lets you to view the put away images on your device.

1. Pick Pictures from the ✳ Assortment.

2. Tap 👁 a photo to view it. To view more photographs or videos, swipe left or right.

• To empower Bixby Vision on the at present shown image, touch Bixby Vision.

• To add the photo to your top selections, press Add to ♡ Top picks.

• To get to the related components, hit ⋮ More choices:

• Subtleties: View and modify the information about the picture.

• Remaster image: To polish a picture, apply programmed picture upgrades.

• Add image impact: Change the slider to make the foundation in your representation photos very substantially visible.

• Duplicate to clipboard: Duplicate the picture, then glue it into an other application.

• Set as backdrop: Set the picture as your PC's experience.

• Move Picture to Get Organizer: Move the photograph into a secure envelope.

• Print: Send the picture to an attached printer.

Adjust photos

Upgrade the presence of your photographs with the modifying gadgets tracked down in the Display.

1. Pick Pictures from the ✳ Assortment.
2. Subsequent to touching a photo to check it, hit ✏ Alter to view the following choices:

   ☀ • Auto change: Utilize programmed acclimations to work on the image.

   ⛶ • Change: Adjust the overall look of the photograph by cutting, twisting, ⊗ flipping, or employing other affects.

   ☼ • Channels: Add variety affects.
   ☺

   • Tone: Change brilliance, distinctiveness, openness, and diverse locations.

   • Beautifications: Add stickers, other piece of art, or written by hand text.

   • More choices: Gain entrance to a more comprehensive scope of changing alternatives.
   • Return: Remove the progressions done to rebuild the initial image.

3. Click Save when you're done.

   Play the video.

View the recordings placed away on your device. Recordings may be favorited and watched comprehensively.

1. Pick Pictures from the ✳ Assortment.
2. Tap a video to view it. To view more photographs or videos, swipe left or right.

• To add the video to your rundown of top choices, hit Add to ♡ Top selections. Under the Collections tab, the video gets added to Top choices.

•To go to the associated highlights, press ⋮ More choices:

- Subtleties: See and change the video's data.
- Open the video player: To observe this video, use the included player.
- Set as foundation picture: Set the video as the background for the lock screen.
- Move to Monitored Organizer: Spot this video within the Safe Envelope.

3. Tap ▶ Play to view the video.

Video brilliance

To observe additional, more distinct tones, boost the video quality.

○ From the Settings menu, pick an option by selecting 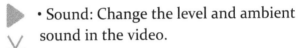 Progressed highlights > Video splendor.

Alter the video

You may alter recordings that are placed away on your device.

1. Choose Pictures from the ✱ Assortment.

2. Tap a video to view it.

3.

Tap Alter to use the following apparatuses:

• Sound: Change the level and ambient sound in the video.

• Play: Press Play to see the edited footage.

• Trim: Eliminate particular video chunks.

• Change: Alter the overall look of the video by editing, twisting, flipping, or employing other affects.

• Channels: Add extra graphics to the video to better enhance it.

• Tone: Change magnificence, diversity, openness, and varied locations.

• Designs: Add stickers, writing, or hand-drawn text.

• More choices: Get near enough to extra changing assets.

• Return: Take out the progressions done to rebuild the initial video.

4. Click "Save," then, at that point "Affirm" when incited.

Send and receive images and Videos.

The Gallery application lets you to exchange recordings and photos.

1. Pick Pictures from the ✳️ Gallery.

2. In the aftermath of picking ⋮ More Choices > Alter, choose the images or recordings you need to share.

3. Tap ⤴ share once you've picked the application or association with utilize to share your selection. Keep the rules.

Dispose of the images and Videos.

Dispose of the motion movies and photographs that are placed away on your gadget.

1. Go to Additional ⋮ choices > ✳️ Gallery> Alter.

2. Tap on the photos and recordings to pick them.

3. When requested, click Yes in the wake of selecting 🗑 Erase.

Consolidate comparable photographs.
In the Display, arrange photos and recordings in light of their degree of comparability.

1. Pick photographs from the ✳️ Gallery, then tap ▢ Group similar images.

2. You may touch ▢ Ungroup related images to come back to the default Gallery view.

Take a screen capture.
Snatch a screen capture of your work area. Your gadget's Exhibition application will therefore build a collection named Screen captures.

○ From any screen, press and delivery the Side and Volume down buttons.

Swipe with your hand to grab a screen capture.

To take a snapshot of the screen, keep your palm in contact with it and swipe the edge over it.

1. From the Settings menu, choose Advanced features> Motions and gestures >. Swipe with your palm to catch.

2. Tap to make this capacity dynamic.

Screen capture settings.

Change the parameters of the screen capture.

○ From the Settings menu, choose Advanced features > Screen captures and screen recorder.

• provide toolbar after catch: In the aftermath of capturing a screen capture, provide more options.
• Erase from the toolbar in the wake of sharing: A screen capture should be subsequently removed after sharing using the toolbar.
• obscure the status and route bars: Make careful to obscure the status and route bars prior to taking a screen shot.
• Design: Pick between exporting your screen shots as JPG or PNG documents.
• Save screen gets: Pick the place in which you desire to preserve your screen grabs.

Option for recording screens

Make a self-representation video using your camera to connect to friends and family, record events on your device, and take notes.

1. From the Quick Settings menu, choose Screen Recorder.

2. Subsequent to choosing a sound decision, hit Record.

3. It starts recording after a three-second beginning. To start recording straight away, essentially press Skip beginning.

• To draw on the screen, press Draw.

• To view a symbol on the screen while employing your S Pen, touch the pointer (Galaxy S24 Ultra as it were).

• To add a forward facing camera recording, press Selfie video.

4. Tap Stop to halt the recording. These soon wind up in the Screen Accounts collection of the Gallery.

Settings for a screen recorder

Control the sound and quality settings of the screen recorder.

○ From the Settings menu, choose ⊙
Advanced features > Screen captures and
screen recorder.

• Utilizing the screen recorder, choose the
noises you desire to capture.

• Select the pixel count for the video quality.
While choosing a higher target for more
obvious quality, more capacity is necessary.

• The selfie video's aspects: Utilize the slider to
modify the video overlay's size.

• Permit the screen to be touched and
interacted during the recording.

• By designating a place to keep your screen
captures, you may "Save screen accounts in."

Chapter Three: Utilizing programs

The programs list displays commonly presented programs, both preloaded and downloaded. Applications may be downloaded by way of the Universe Store and the Google Play™ store.

○ Swipe the screen up to see the Applications list from a Home screen.

Switch off or delete the app.

Introduced apps may be deleted from your device. You may handicap some preinstalled programs that are available on your mobile phone naturally. Debilitated programs are shut off and hidden away from view.

○ From the Applications menu, contact and hold a program, then choose Uninstall/Handicap.

Look for applications.

On the off chance that you are don't know where to seek for a program or arrangement, use the Hunt option.

1. From the Applications menu, pick Hunt and input a word or words. As you write, results for appropriate settings and applications come up on the screen.

2. Tap a result to open that application.

🔆 Counsel: You may adjust the pursuit bounds by clicking More options > Settings.

Sort the apps.

You may select to present application simple paths consecutively or in a custom game design.

○ Sendoff Applications and select ⋮ More >. Sort in light of the following possibilities for arranging:
• Modify the request for the apps the hard way.
• Orchestrate apps in consecutive request.

🔆 Counsel: Tap More choices > to remove empty symbol spaces when physically asking applications (Custom request). Organize the pages.

Create and use folders.

To arrange application simple routes on the Applications list, construct folders.

1. You may drag an application alternative route from the Applications menu over another application simple route to showcase it.

2. To create the envelope, discharge the program different manner.
   • Dole out a name to the organizer.

89

( ) • Range: Change the folder colour.

✚ • Incorporate applications: Extend the folder with other projects. Press the applications you need to employ, then, at that point, touch Done.

3. Tap ⟨ Back to close the envelope.

Move an folder to the Home screen.
Replicating a folder to the home screen is doable.

○ In the Applications rundown, contact and hold an envelope, then, at that point, select

⊕ Add to Home.

Erase an envelope
At the time where an envelope is deleted, the application simple routes reappear in the Applications list.

1. Contact and hold an organizer from Applications to delete it.

2. In the aftermath of choosing 🗑 "Erase Folder," click "Yes" when challenged.

A Game Booster
Mess about at your greatest pace, based upon the quantity you utilize. To further enrich

your game experience, empower includes and incapacitate notices.

○ While in a game, swipe up from the bottom portion of the screen to get at the route bar. The associated selections are on the extreme left and right sides:

• Touch protection: Lock the screen to avoid inadvertent tapping. This is the decision that is selected spontaneously.

• Game Enhancer: Extra features that may be built encompass execution observing and hindering screen contacts, portrayals, and the menu bar.

The application's settings
Organize the downloaded and introduced applications.

○ From the Settings menu, choose Applications. Tapping a configurable option indicates your decision:
• Pick default applications: Pick which projects to open for chatting, calling, sending messages, and that's only the beginning.
• Samsung application settings: View a rundown of the programs that are open and alter their settings.
• Applications you use: Tap an application to examine and alter its protection and usage

settings. Each application provides fascinating layout alternatives.

Guidance: To restore lately updated application settings, select ⋮ More options > Reset application preferences.

Chapter Four: Samsung Apps

Samsung programming.

The following programs can be preinstalled or be downloaded over-the-air to your device throughout configuration. Applications may be downloaded by way of the World Store and the Google Play™store. Specialist co-ops might introduce a variety of choices.

AR Zone

You may get to the whole of your Augmented Reality (AR) highlights from a single area.

Bixby

Bixby offers stuff that is tailor suited to you in view of your affiliations. Bixby leverages your usage examples to offer stuff you may regard as intriguing.

Galaxy Store

Search for and obtain premium apps that are merely feasible with World contraptions. All that may be downloaded from the World Store needs a Samsung account.

Galaxy Wearable

To coordinate your device with your Samsung Watch, apply this program.

Game Launcher

Your games will be all accordingly arranged in one area.

> Counsel: If the Applications list doesn't display Game Launcher, choose Advanced features > Game Launcher from the Settings menu, and thereafter tap .

PENUP

Scan the internet for goods to add to your collection, transmit images, or provide opinions on others' efforts (but only Galaxy S24 Ultra). All people who utilize the S Pen to paint, doodle, scribble, or draw are joined by this gathering.

Samsung Free

Get free entrance to clever games, news and articles from a breadth of sources, and live television.

Samsung Global Goals

Find more about the Worldwide Objectives program and utilize this application's advertising to contribute to organizations that promote these causes.

Samsung Members

With your System mobile phone, achieve more and receive more. Utilize portion merely occasions and material, as well as Do-It-Yourself assistance assets. Samsung Individuals may now be stacked on your mobile phone, or you may download and introduce them from the Universe or Google Play shops.

Samsung TV Plus

Benefit from free news, pleasure, and more on your Samsung television and smart phones.

Samsung Wallet

Samsung Wallet lets you to make installments using your device. You may use your charge card any place you can swipe or press it. To employ Samsung Pay, you need have a record.

Smart Switch

Utilize Brilliant Change to relocate contacts, images, and various papers from your previous mobile phone.

SmartThings

By regulating, robotizing, and inspecting your house temperature from a mobile phone, SmartThings enables you to modify it to your specific wants. You may interface various devices instantly or each gadget in turn with the product. Really look at the condition with your contraptions by examining the dashboard out.

Note: Mistakes or faults in non-Samsung connected gadgets are not protected by the Samsung guarantee; contact the producer of the non-Samsung gadget for support.

Tips

See the client handbook for your device and a few basic suggestions and deceives.

**Calculator**

The Mini-computer program delivers fundamental and logical numerical skills with a unit converter.

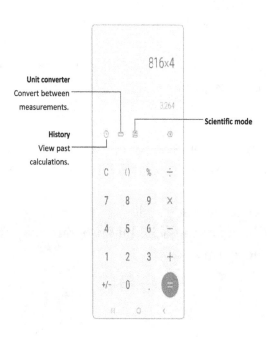

 Calendar

By linking the Schedule program to any one of your multiple web-based accounts, you can synchronize each of your schedules in a single area.

Add calendars

You may add your accounts to the Calendar app.

1. ☰ Navigation drawer may be selected from the Calendar 🔟 menu.

2. Tapping Manage calendars > Add ✛ account will allows you to specify an account type.

3. Enter your account data and adhere to the requirements.

🔆 Guidance: Records may likewise comprise contacts, email, and other abilities.

Schedule ready style

Clients of the Schedule program may change the alarm style.

1. Select ☰ Navigation drawer > ⚙ Calendar settings > Alert style from the 🔲 Calendar menu.

The selections that are available are as per the following:

• Light: There's a brief blare and a sound warning.

• Medium: A succinct sound and a full-screen alert are presented.

• Solid: A full-screen warning and ring sound will be perceptible after you excuse it.

2. The alarm style that was recently picked will figure out which of the following sound options is accessible:

• Short sound: Select the warning sound for the Medium or Light readiness classes.

• Long sound: Pick the alarm sound for Serious regions of strength for the kind.

Make an event
If it's not too much hassle, employ your timetable to create occasions.

1. To make an event from the 🔲 Calendar, tap to ⊕ add an event.

2. Click Save once the occasion's subtleties have been inserted.

Dispose an event

Erase occasions from your Schedule.

1. Tap an occurrence from the again to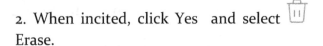
Calendar to edit it.

2. When incited, click Yes and select ⦗🗑⦘
Erase.

Clock

The Clock program features timekeeping and
morning timer highlights.

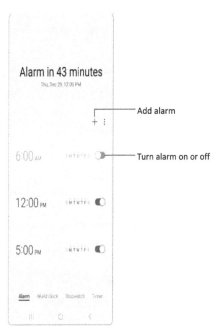

Alarm

100

Utilize the Caution option to set up warnings and establish one-time or ongoing alerts.

1. Select ✛ add alarm from ◉ Clock.

2. To set an alarm, tap any of the adjacent buttons:
• Time: Pick a timeframe the alarm.
• Day: Pick which days you feel this alarm should ring.
• Name the alarm: Give the alarm a name.
• Alarm sound: Pick an alarm sound and apply the slider to modify the alarm's volume.
• Vibration: Pick whether to cause the alarm to vibrate.
• Snooze: Grant snoozing. Set the alarm on intervals and repeat and while snoozing.

2. Tap Save to keep up with the alarm.

Guidance: Tap ⋮ More options > Set sleep mode schedule to input your sleep routine, set up a sleep time reminder, and have your device fall into rest mode naturally.

Dispose an alarm
You may pull down an alert that you've put up.

1. Press and hold one of the ◉ clock's alarms.

2. Touch ⬚ Delete button.

Setups for Alerts

It is doable to arrange the device to vibrate for clocks and alarms, regardless or not the Sound mode is set to Quiet or Vibrate.

1. Pick Settings under ⦂ more options from the ⊙ Clock menu.

2. At the point when the system sound is off, hit Silence alarms to activate.

Alarm settings

You receive notifications when an alert is likely to go off.

1. Pick Settings under⦂ More options from the ⊙ Clock app.

2. Tap upcoming alarm notification to set the minutes till an upcoming alarm.

World clock

The World Clock lets you to observe the time in various metropolitan regions globally.

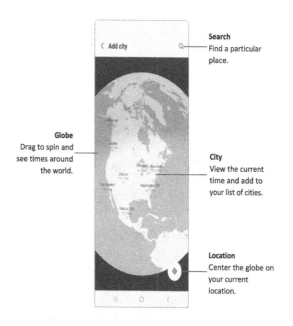

Search
Find a particular place.

Globe
Drag to spin and see times around the world.

City
View the current time and add to your list of cities.

Location
Center the globe on your current location.

1. From the 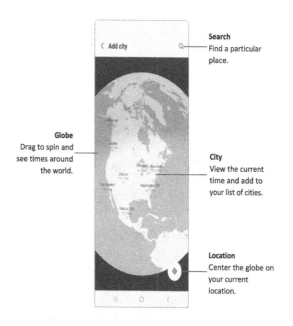 Clock, pick World clock.

2. Pick the ╋ city.

3. Pivot the globe by tossing it, then, at that point, tap the perfect city and choose Add.
• To delete a city, touch and hold it, then choose 🗑 Erase.

Time zone converter
To figure out the neighborhood times in various urban communities on your rundown, write down a point in time in

one of the urban locations on your Reality clock list.

1. From 🔘 Clock, choose World Clock.

2. Under ⋮ more options, choose Time zone converter.

3. Tap ▼ Menu to choose another city.

　　• To add a city for the list, hit ┼ Add city.

3. Swipe the hours, minutes, and period (AM or PM) of the clock to set a time. Local times for other cities are   updated by default

• To restore the clock to the ongoing time, hit Reset.

Weather settings
Show weather information on your international watch.

1. From 🔘Clock, choose World Clock.

2. Tap ⋮ More options > Settings > Show weather to turn on or off the weather data.
3. Tap Temperature to shift over from Fahrenheit to Celsius.

Stopwatch
The stopwatch lets you to timing situations to the closest 100th of a second.

1. Pick Stopwatch from the ⊙ Clock menu.
2. Tap Start to begin timing.
   • Tap Lap to check your lap timings.
3. Tap Stop to terminate the timing.
   • After the clock has paused, hit Resume to begin timing.
   • To reset the Stopwatch, hit Reset.

Timer.
Set a commencement clock for 99 hours, 59 minutes, and 59 seconds.

1. Tap ⊙ Clock to pick Timer.

2. Utilize the keypad to set the timer by pressing Hours, Minutes, and Seconds.

3. Tap Start to begin the Timer.
   • Tap Respite to pause the Clock temporarily. To continue, hit the Resume button.
   • Press Erase to drop and reset the time.

Preset timer
Make a clock and save it.

1. From the ⊙ Clock menu, click Timer>
⋮ More options > Add preset clock.

2. Enter a name for the timer and the duration.

3. Tap Add to save the timer.

• Select ⋮ More options > edit preset timers, to edit a previously saved preset timer.

Timer options
There is an option to alter the Clock.

1. Pick Timer from the 🕐 Clock menu.

2. Select Settings from the ⋮ More options menu.

• Sound: Utilize the inbuilt timer sound or record your own.

• Vibration: Set the timer to vibrate.

• Display a mini timer: The timer appears as a pop-up window when you restrict the Clock application.

Other settings
Examine and modify the Clock instrument's settings.

o Select ⋮ More options > Settings from the 🕐 Clock menu.

• Permissions: Review the mandatory and optional permissions listed in the Clock application.

106

• Customization Service: Access your Samsung account to customize specific content in supported apps

• Contact us: To get in touch with Samsung support, use Samsung Members.

• About Clock: Verify updates and display the most recent version of the software.

Contacts

Organize and manage your connections. You can sync with individual files that you have loaded onto your device. Additionally, accounts may support email, schedules, and other features.

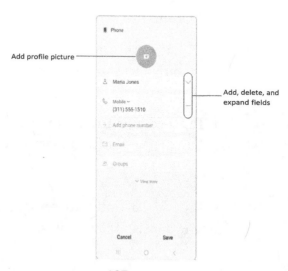

Establish a contact

1. Select ✛ "Make contact" from the 👤 Contacts menu.
2. After entering the contact's details, click Save.

Edit a contact

You can modify an existing field or add new ones to a contact's data rundown by pushing on it.

1. From the list of contacts 👤 , pick a contact.

2. Press Edit. ✎
3. To add, change or remove information, tap any of the field.
4. Select "Save."

Favourites

The contacts you value the most are efficiently accessible from various apps and appear first in your contact list.

1. Tap a contact from Contacts 👤.
2. Select Favourites to mark a contact as a favourite ☆ .

• Tap ★ Favorites to remove a contact from your list of favourites.

Share a contact

Use a variety of sharing tools and services to share a contact with other people.

1. Tap a contact from 👤 Contacts.

2. Press the 🔗 "Share" button.

3. Select text or vCard file (VCF).

4. Choose a sharing tool and proceed as directed.

💡 Advice: While viewing a contact, select ⋮ More > QR code to quickly share contact information with friends and family. As a result, whenever you modify the contact data boxes, the QR code is updated.

Display content when sharing contacts

Any application allows you to directly share content with your contacts. Your occasionally used contacts appear in the share window once enacted.

o Select ⊕ Advanced options from Settings > Show contacts while sharing content. Tap ◯▶ to enable the component.

Groups
Organize your contacts with groups.

Create a group
Create your own contact groups.

1. Navigate to the ⊙ Contacts menu and choose Groups from the ☰ Navigation menu.
2. Click Create group, after entering information about the group.
  • Assigned a name to the newly formed group.
  • Set a distinctive tone for the group with the "Group ringtone."
  • Add members: Click Done after selecting which contacts to include in the new group.
3. Select "Save."

Including or removing contacts from group
Expand a group's contact list or remove existing ones.

○ From the ⑧ Contacts menu, select ☰ Show navigation menu > Groups. Next, choose a groups.

• Press and hold the contact to 🗑 delete it.

• Select ✎ Edit > Add members, and then select the required contacts to be added. After finished, select Done > Save.

Deliver a message to a group.
Instantaneously message each member of the group.

1. Select Show ☰ navigation menu > Groups from the ⑧ Contacts menu, then choose a group.
2. Select More options > Express your thought.

Use email to stay in contact with a group.
Send each member of the group an email.

1. Select Show ☰ navigation menu > Group from the ⑧ Contacts menu, then choose a group.

2. Select More options > Send Mail.

3. To choose every contact, click the All checkbox located at the top of the screen, or tap each contact one at a time. Next, tap Done

• Only the individuals gathered whose data includes an email address are displayed.

4. Select an email address and adhere to the instructions.

Delete a group
Delete a group you created.

1. Select Show ☰ navigation menu > select Groups from the 🔵 Contacts menu, then choose a group.

2. Select More options > Delete group.

• Press Delete group only, if you just want to delete only the group.

• To delete the group and remove the participants and their contacts, tap Delete group and move members them to the trash.

Manage Contacts
A single contact record can be created by connecting a few contacts together, and contacts can be imported or exchanged.

Connect with contacts

Join passages together to consolidate contact information from multiple sources into a single contact.

Choose Show ≡ navigation menu > Manage contacts from the 🧑 Contacts menu.

1. Contacts with duplicate phone numbers, names, and email addresses are typically recorded collectively when you choose "Merge contacts."

2. After selecting the contacts by tapping on them, select Merge.

Import contacts
Contacts can be imported to your phone as vCard Files (VCF).

1. Choose Show ≡ navigation menu > Manage contacts from the 🧑 Contacts menu.

2. Select Import contacts and adhere to the instructions.

Export Contacts

From your device, send contacts as vCard files (VCF).

1. Choose Show ☰ navigation menu > Manage contacts from the 👤 Contacts menu.

2. Select Product contacts and adhere to the instructions.

Align contacts.
Ensure that every contact in every account has been updated.

1. Choose Show ☰ navigation menu > Manage contacts from the 👤 Contacts menu.

2. Get things going in the sync button.

Delete contacts.
Get rid of a contact or several contacts.

1. You can select which contacts to erase by tapping on them.

   • Tapping and holding a contact will also allow you to select it.

3. When prompted, confirm by tapping

    Delete

Emergency contacts
You can still call your crisis contacts even if your cell phone is locked.

○ Select 🔺Safety and emergency > Emergency contacts from the Settings menu.

• Include a member: Prepare a list of phone numbers to have on hand in case of emergency.

• Show on the lock screen: You can easily contact crisis contacts in an emergency by placing them on the lock screen.

◉ Internet

Samsung Web is a reliable, speedy, and user-friendly web browser for your device. You can enjoy faster surfing, increased security protection, and enhanced reading capabilities with safer Web browsing options.

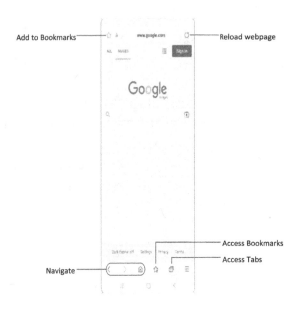

Add to Bookmarks

Reload webpage

Access Bookmarks

Access Tabs

Navigate

Program tabs:

You can view multiple site pages instantly with tabs.

○ Select Open from the ◉ Web under Tabs ①.

• Select ① Tabs > ✕ Close tab to end a tab.

Create a Favorite

Try saving your top pages as bookmarks for easy access.

○ Select ☆ Save as a bookmark from the ◖ Web to store the currently open page.

Get an Open Bookmark
Open a webpage effectively from the Bookmarks page.

1. Select �Bookmarks from the ◖ Internet by clicking.

2.

2. Click on a bookmark connect.

Maintain a webpage on your website.
There are multiple options within the Samsung Web application for storing a webpage.

○ Select ☰ Devices > Add page to from the Web to view the options below:

• Bookmarks: Include the URL in your collection of favorite websites.

• Basic access: See a list of the websites you frequently visit or bookmark.

• Home screen: Create a simple path from your Home screen to the website page.

• Saved pages: Save the content of web pages to your device in case you get disconnected.

Analyze each experience group separately.

To view a summary of recently visited website pages,

Choosing ☰ Devices > History via the Web menu is applicable.

Use the shortcut Snap ⋮ More > to remove the experiences from your program. a transparent past.

Share webpages
You can recommend websites to people you know.
● Select Instruments > Offer from the Web, then adhere to the headings displayed on the screen.

Covert mode
Pages that are found in covert mode do not show up in your search or program history, nor do they leave any treats or other follower history on your device. Regular tab windows are more subdued in tone than secret tabs.

Any files you download remain on your device even after you close the enigmatic tab.

1. Select the Enable Secret mode under 🔲 Tabs.

2. To start the Mysterious method of reading, click Start.

Configurations for covert modes
Use a biometric lock or secret phrase to go into Secret mode.

1. From the ⬤ website page, choose 🔲 Tabs.

2. The accompanying boundaries can be selected by selecting ⋮ More choices > Secret mode settings:

 • Use a secret word/ password: In order to access Secret mode and utilize biometrics, you must combine a secret key.

 • Clear all data and go back to the original configurations to reset Secret mode.

Turn off the covert setting.
Turn off Secret mode and resume your regular browsing.

○ Select 🔲 Tabs > Turn off Secret functionality.

Web settings

Modify the Web application's connection settings.

- ○ Select ≡ Devices > Web to access the Settings menu.

Messages

Use the Messages app to stay in touch with your contacts by sending them greetings, pictures, and emoticons. Expert cooperatives may present a range of options.

○ From 💬 Messages, tap ○ Compose new message

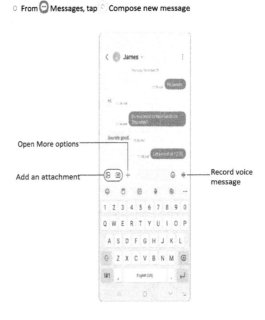

Messages of inquiry

To quickly locate a message, use the inquiry highlight.

1. Select ⌕ "Search" within 💬 Messages.
2. Enter your search terms in the field and press the console's ⌕ "Search" button.

End the conversation.
By stopping the conversation, you can remove your collection of changed experiences.

1. Select the 🗑 Erase option found in the 💬 Messages menu's Additional options ⋮.
2. Simply tap it to end a visit.
3. Select "Erase all," and then respond "Yes" when prompted.

Messages during an emergency
Tell your crisis contacts something specific using audio and visuals.

○ Select 🔔 Crisis SOS under Wellbeing and crisis from the Settings menu. Five Side key presses will initiate the accompanying activities.

121

• Start: Ascertain the number of seconds that ought to elapse before executing a crisis maneuver.

• Make a crisis call: Decide which number to call after reaching a crisis resolution.

• Sharing information with crisis contacts: Allow your crisis contacts to be aware of your whereabouts.

Counsel: Pressing and holding the Side and Volume down keys while selecting Crisis call will also launch Crisis SOS.

Emergency sharing
Tell your crisis contacts something specific using audio and visuals.

1. Select Wellbeing and crisis > Crisis sharing from the Settings menu. Choose what, if you truly want help, to send off to your crisis contacts:

• Attach photos: Use your front and rear cameras to snap and send photos.

• Play the sound recording and share a five-second sample that you were able to capture.

2. Select the media and click "Start crisis sharing" to forward it to your crisis contacts.

Settings for messages
Set up the boundaries for the text and mixed-media correspondence.

○ Select ⋮ More choices > Settings from the 💬 menu.

Crisis alerts
Crisis precautions alert you to certain situations despite possible risks. An emergency notification may be sent.

   ○ To change the alarms you receive, select Remote Emergency alerts > ⚠️Wellbeing and Crisis from the Settings menu.

   💡 Advice: Exhortation Notices are another way to access crisis alerts.

Select notifications > 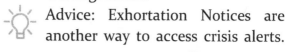High level Settings > Remote Crisis Cautions from the Settings menu.

My Files
View and manage the documents that are stored on your device, including images,

videos, audio files, and recordings. Additionally, you have access to and control over the data stored in your cloud accounts.

Search

Storage locations
Additional locations, such as cloud accounts, are displayed here if supported.

Keep track of meetings
The following groups are created from the records on the device:
• Examine the documents that have recently received visits.
This option will show up if at least one record has been admitted after the deadline.

124

• Classes: Arrange your documents according to their particular type.

• Capacity: Access data stored in cloud accounts and on your device.

- Cloud accounts change based on the authentication systems you use.

• Examine your space: Determine what takes up the most space.

My Files' designs

To change the executive's settings for your record, go to My Files. But that's just the beginning. A range of choices could be introduced by specialized organizations.

o Select ⋮ Additional options > Settings from ⬜ My Files to view the related choices:

• Cloud accounts: Manage and maintain sufficient proximity to your cloud-based assets.

• Documentation: Handle document entry, erasure, and display.

• Examine capacity: Select the record size that will draw attention when scanning capacity.

• Privacy: Carefully review the consents in My Documents.

Call

The Phone app provides a history of previous calls. Examine the highlights of the high-level calling. Get in touch with your specialized organization to learn more. The Phone application interface and elements that are accessible vary amongst specialized cooperatives.

Phone Calls

Using the Contacts tab, Home screen, Recents tab, and other features of the Phone application, you can decide and make decisions.

Reach a decision.

You could choose and make choices from your phone's Home screen.

Enter a number on the keypad located under "Telephone" and select "Call."

• If the keypad is not visible, press Keypad.

Decide over the phone with someone in Recents.

The call log lists all incoming, outgoing, and missed calls.

1. To view a list of recent calls, use the Telephone menu and select Recents.

2. After you've tapped a contact, choose Call.

Utilize Contacts to make a phone call selection.

Use the Contacts application to decide on a phone call.

○ To decide from the right, swipe your finger across a contact in Contacts.

Take a call.

When a call is received, the phone rings and displays the name or number of the visitor. The impending hit shows up as a pop-up screen if, by chance, you are using an application.

○ To respond, drag 📞 Reply to one side on the screen that appears when a call is received.

🔆 Advice: Click 📞 Reply on the pop-up screen that appears when a call comes in.

Turn down a call
Rejecting incoming calls is a choice you make. The impending hit shows up as a pop-up screen if, by chance, you are using an application.

○ Drag the ⌒ Decline button to one side on the incoming call screen to end the call and send it to your voicemail.

🔆 Advice: To end the call and send it to your phone message, choose ⬤ Decline on the upcoming pop-up screen.

Turn down with a note
You can choose to message someone in response to an incoming call.

○ Select a message by dragging it vertically from the incoming call screen.

Counsel : a pop-up screen appears when a call comes through. Choose a message, then click Send.

Cut off a call

When you're prepared to end the call, press ⬤ End call.

Activities One Can Do While Talking on the Phone

While on the phone, you can accomplish multiple tasks, swap between speakers and a headset, and adjust the call volume.

To adjust the volume, simply press the Volume keys.

Switch to a speaker or headset.

Be mindful of the speaker's approach or use a Bluetooth® headset (not included).

○ Press ◁)) Speaker to listen to the guest through a speaker; press ✳ Bluetooth to use a Bluetooth headset to listen to the guest.

Multitask

Your live call appears in the Status bar in the unlikely event that you navigate away from the call screen to use another app.

To return to the call screen;

o Drag the Status bar down to access the Warning board.

In order to conclude a call while multitasking,
After pulling down the Status bar to reveal the Warning board, hit 😐 End call.

Call backgrounds
Choose a picture or a video to play while making decisions.

o To view the associated settings, select ⋮
More options > Settings > Call background from the 🅒 Telephone menu.
• Format: Select the appearance of the person's profile picture when call data is displayed.
• Base: Select an image to display while using a phone.

Call pop-up settings.
Calls may occur as pop-up windows while you're working on other projects.

○ Select ⋮ More options > Settings > Call display while using applications from the 🅲 Telephone menu. The options that are available are as follows:

- Full screen: The Telephone application will display an incoming call in full screen mode.

- Small pop-up: Display a tiny spring up at the top of the screen whenever a call is received.

- Mini pop-up: Display a more subdued spring up when a call comes in.

- Keep calls in pop-up: Enable this feature to continue bringing up the spring up window after a response has been given.

Manage calls
A call log contains your call histories. You can use phone messaging, block numbers, and set up speed dials.

Call history
The call log contains a record of the phone numbers you have called, received, and missed.

o Select Recents via 🅲 Phone. There is a list of late calls displayed. The

131

name of the guest will appear if they are in your Contacts list.

Save a contact of a recent caller.
You can update or add contacts to your Contacts list by using the information from a new call.

1. From the Telephone menu, select Recent.

2. After you tap the call that contains the information you need to save in your Contacts list, choose Add to Contacts.

3. To change an existing contact or add a new one, make the appropriate selection.

Get rid of call history.
In order to remove something from the call log:

1. Select Recent from the phone.
2. Holding down on the perfect call will remove it from the call log.
3. Hover over the Delete icon.

Block a phone number

If you add a guest to your block show, you can attempt to block that number from future voice or message messages.

1. Select Recents from ⓒ phone.
2. After selecting the contact you want to add to the Block list, select ⓞ Details.

3. Next, select ⃠ Block from the menu ⦂ or More > Block contact, then hit the right button.

☀ Counsel: Under Settings, you can also modify your Block list. You can select ⦂ More options > Settings > Block numbers from the ⓒ Telephone menu.

Fast dial

A contact can be given the ability to conveniently call their default number by setting an easy route number to them.

1. Select Keypad > ⦂ More options > Speed dial numbers from the ⓒ Telephone menu. The held speed dial numbers are displayed on the Speed dial numbers screen.

2. Press any random number.

133

• To select a different Speed dial number from the ones that appear next in the progression, tap ▼ Menu.

• Voice messaging is the primary use case for number one.

3. To link a contact with the number, select 👤 Add from Contacts or type in a name or number.

• In the Speed dial number box, the selected contact appears.

Use the fast dial to reach a make a call.
Speed Dial allows you to make phone call.

o   Select the Speed dial number on the 🔵 phone and hold it down.

• If there are more than three digits in the Speed dial number, enter the first three and hold the last digit.

Take out a speed dial number.
Once a Speed dial number has been assigned, it can be removed.

1. Go to ⋮ More options > Speed dial numbers from the 🔵 Telephone menu.

2. After selecting the reach you want to remove from Speed dial, tap ➖ Erase.

Emergency/ Crisis Calls

No matter your phone network status, you can still call the local crisis number. In the unlikely event that your phone is off, you can make snap decisions.

1. After selecting (C) Telephone and entering the crisis number (911 in North America), select Call.
2. Finish the call. For this kind of call, you can make use of most of the in-call highlights.

Advice: If your phone is locked, anyone can use it to contact for help in an emergency at night by dialing the crisis number on it. The crisis calling highlight is the only option available to the guest when the screen is locked. The phone is still under constant observation.

Phone settings
By using these options, you can modify the Telephone application's settings.

○ Select Settings > ⋮ More choices from the (C) Telephone menu.

135

Discretionary phone services
Your remote specialist co-op and administration plan may cover the following calling services.

Make a multi-party call.
While you're on the phone, you can make another call. Expert cooperatives may present a range of options.

1. To dial the next number, click Add ┼ call from the current call.

2. You can move between the 📞 two calls by answering the first one by
    • Pressing the On Hold or Swap number. After entering the new number, select "Call."
 • Press "Merge to multi-gathering" to instantly hear both calls.

Video conversations
To start a video call,

Tap 🅒 phone, enter a number and select

🎥 Meet or 📹 Video call or 🅒 Video call.

Note: Not every device can make video calls. The recipient can choose to accept the video call or respond to it by speaking on the phone normally.

Video conversations effects
When participating in a video discussion, you have the option to alter or dim your experience using the various applications.

1. Select ⬤ Progressed highlights > Video call impacts from the Settings menu.
2. Press ⬤ to activate this feature.
3. Select a useful configuration:

Base tone: Based on your surrounding conditions, your virtual landscape will subsequently change to a strong variety.

Foundation picture: Choose an image from your library to serve as the background of your video call.

Wi-Fi calls
Once you're a connected to a Wi-Fi network, you can use Wi-Fi to make calls.

1. Select ⁝ More options > Settings > Wi-Fi calling from the ⬤ Phone menu.

2. Press ⬤ to make use of features.

137

3. Follow the instructions to configure and set up Wi-Fi calling.

Real Time Text (RTT)
While on a call, type back and forth with the other person nonstop.

When on a with someone whose phone is either connected to a teletypewriter (TTY) or has RTT capabilities, you can use RTT. Every incoming RTT call displays the RTT symbol.

1. Choose Settings under ⋮Additional choices on the 🅒 Phone menu.

2. The accompanying settings can be viewed and altered by tapping the ongoing text:

    • RTT call button: Adjust how easily the button can be seen.

      - Only visible during calls: It should only be possible to see the RTT call button when on a call.

      - Constantly visible: During calls and on the keypad,

the RTT call button should always be visible.

- Use an external TTY console: Make sure the RTT console is hidden when utilizing an external TTY console.
- TTY mode: Choose your preferred TTY mode from the console. Samsung Medical

Samsung Health

Rest, nutrition, and physical activity are just a few aspects of your daily life that you can monitor and manage with Samsung Health™.

Note: The information compiled from Samsung Health, this device, or associated content is not meant to be used for diagnosing infections or other conditions, nor for treating, curing, preventing, or relieving illnesses.

Various factors, such as the environment in which it is used or worn, specific exercises done while wearing it, the gadget's settings, client design and data provided by the client, and opposite end-client communications, can affect the accuracy of data and information provided by this device and its related programming.

Before starting a fitness regimen
Even though the Samsung Haelth app is a fantastic addition to your daily routine, it is always advisable to consult your primary care physician before beginning any new wellness program.

While most people can safely engage in moderately active work, such as brisk walking, clinical experts advise speaking with your PCP before starting an exercise program, particularly if you have diabetes, asthma, lung disease, liver or kidney illness, joint pain, cardiac illness, or any other condition.

Before beginning an exercise program, consult your primary care physician (PCP) if you experience any of the following side effects:

- pain or discomfort in your arms, neck, chest, or jaw when exercising;
- confusion or disorientation;
- dyspnea during light exertion, when you lie down, or when you wake up;

- swelling in your lower legs, especially in the evenings;
- a pounding or racing heartbeat;
- or pain in your muscles that goes away when you relax.

It is advised that you speak with your PCP or another healthcare provider before starting an exercise program. Before starting another activity program, you should consult your PCP if you are pregnant, have multiple medical conditions, or are unsure of your current state of health.

Samsung Notes

You can take voice notes, text notes, photos with captions, and music notes with Samsung Notes. With places for interpersonal interaction, sharing your notes is easy.

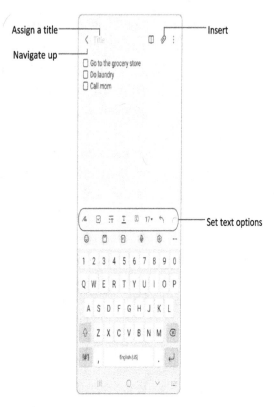

Assign a title

Navigate up

Insert

Set text options

Make a note.

Include text, images, audio recordings, and more.

1. Choose Add from Samsung Notes.

2. Make content by utilizing the text's choices.

Audio recordings

Record voice notes that can be interpreted and used in meetings or educational settings. While you record the clamors, take notes. The text comparison appears in sync with the playback.

1. Click ✏️ Add from 📋 Samsung Notes.

2. Keep the 📎 Voice Recording button depressed.

3. While the sound is being recorded, use the text selections to create content.

Modify notes.
Make changes to the notes you take.

1. To view a note in 📋 Samsung Notes, tap on it.

2. Press ✏️ Edit, then make your edits from there.

3. When you're finished, select Explore up.

Observes options
It is possible to organize, manage, and alter notes.

  o The highlights that go with it are

    provided by 📋 Samsung Notes:

    • 📄 Import PDF: Use
  Samsung   Notes to open a PDF
         🔍 document.
         ⋮

• Search: Look up a particular phrase.

• Alternative options:

- Change: Decide which notes to copy, remove, lock, make available, or store in a file.
- View: Choose between a basic rundown, framework, or rundown.

- Arrange your top selections according to the most important need: The notes you have favorited will be at the top of the main page.

Notes sections
Your notes are viewable by category.
Select the ≡ Show route menu option from ⬛Samsung Notes to view the decisions that were made underneath:

⚙ • Settings: Navigate to the Samsung Notes application's settings.
• All note: Examine each and every note.
• Shared journals: Log in to your Samsung account to see notepads that you have shared with your contacts.

• Trash: View notes that have been deleted for a maximum of 15 days.

• Folder: See remarks in groups.

• Increase, decrease, and manage folders under the board organizer.

Google software

The Google apps that go with it could have already been installed on your phone. New apps may be released via the Google Play™ store.

 Chrome

Use Chrome™ to browse the web and sync your address bar data, open tabs, and bookmarks from your PC to your mobile device.

 Drive

You may share, access, rename, and view documents stored in your cloud account on Google Drive.

 Gmail

Use the online email management tool provided by Google to send and receive messages.

 Google

Utilize tools to find happiness on the internet based on your preferences. To view information that has been modified for you, activate your personalized feed.

 Google TV

Watch movies and TV shows that you have paid for on Google Play. On your device, you may also see recordings that have been stored.

 Maps

Obtain headlines and more information relevant to the region. To use Google Guides, you must provide permission to local governments.

 Meet

Utilize video visit on several platforms, such as tablets, smartphones, smart devices, and the internet.

 Messages

Send direct messages using Google Visit to those who have the ability to notify others about information or Wi-Fi.

 Photos

As a result, you may use Google Photos™ to back up and save your images and videos to your Google Record.

 Play Store

Look through the Google Play store to discover fresh video games, novels, periodicals, soundtracks, movies, and TV shows.

 Wallet

Use Google Wallet to make payments with your Android phone at participating retailers and mobile apps.

YouTube

On your device, you may view and share YouTube™ recordings.

YT Music

Go to YouTube Music to listen to music, look through playlists, and find experts.

Microsoft apps
On your device, the accompanying Microsoft programs may come pre-installed. Both the Google Play Store and the Universe Store provide applications for download.

Outlook

Contacts, tasks, calendars, emails, and much more can all be accessed with Outlook.

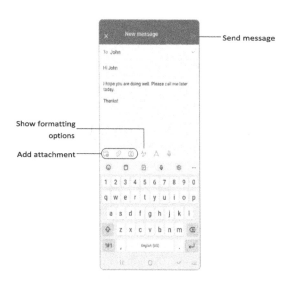

Send message

Show formatting options

Add attachment

Microsoft 365

With the Microsoft 365 app, enjoy Word, Succeed, and PowerPoint on your smartphone.

OneDrive

With your free online OneDrive® record, you may save and share documents, audio files, images, and more. Generally, you may access your record via a computer, tablet, or smartphone.

Chapter Five: Settings

Configurations

Obtain Preferences

There are many methods for accessing your device's settings.

•Swipe down from the Home screen and choose ⚙ Settings.

• Click ◉ Settings, From Apps.

Find the Settings.

In the unlikely event that you are unsure of a setting's exact location, you may search for it.

1. Choose 🔍 Search from the Settings menu to start creating keywords.
2. To increase that setting, tap a paragraph.

Connections

Handle the connections your device makes with other devices and other companies.

Wi-Fi

Connecting your device to a Wi-Fi network allows you to access the Internet without using your mobile data.

1. Select Connections > Wi-Fi from the Settings menu by clicking. Next, push to activate Wi-Fi and search for organizations.

2. When prompted, choose an organization and input a secret word.

3. Select "Associate" from the menu.

Connect to a hidden wireless network .
If a sweep is unable to locate the perfect Wi-Fi organization, you may still associate by manually inputting its information. Before you begin, find out the identity and secret word from the Wi-Fi network director.

1. Navigate to Connections > Wi-Fi in the Settings menu and tap to activate Wi-Fi.

2. You may choose it by tapping the Add network option located at the bottom of the list.

3. Provide specifics about the distant organization:

o Network name: Fill in this form with the actual name of the company.

- Security: Choose a security option from the menu and input the passcode as needed.
- Password: Type the code word for the network here.
- Counting a network that is clandestine is recommended.
- See also: Make sense of other confusing designs, such as interim settings and IP.
4. Select "Save."

Advice: Scan ⬚ a QR code with your device's camera to map a Wi-Fi network by touching the Sweep QR code.

Wi-Fi Direct
Wi-Fi Direct allows for the exchange of information between devices over Wi-Fi.

1. Navigate to 🛜 connections > Wi-Fi in the Settings menu and tap ⬭ to turn on Wi-Fi.

2. Select Wi-Fi Direct under ⋮ More from the menu.

3. To establish an association, tap a device and follow the on-screen instructions. Remove the Wi-Fi Direct add-on.

Keep your device away from anything that has Wi-Fi Direct enabled.

- o From the Settings menu, choose 📶connections > Wi-Fi > More options > Wi-Fi Direct. To deactivate a device, tap it.

Intelligent Wi-Fi settings

You may manage stored organizations, connect to various Wi-Fi networks and hotspots, and check your device's organization address. Expert cooperatives may provide a range of options.

1. Navigate to 📶Connections > Wi-Fi in the Settings menu and tap ⬭ to turn on Wi-Fi.

2. Click ⋮ More options > Canny Wi-Fi to see the related options:

- o If all else is equal, use portable data: If enabled, your device will continuously use portable data in the event that your Wi-Fi connection is unstable. It returns to WiFi at the point when the signal strength is stable.
- o Switch to more dependable Wi-Fi networks: Make the switch by yourself

154

to dependable or faster Wi-Fi networks.

- Wi-Fi auto-side road or auto-on: Enable Wi-Fi in areas you often visit.
- Display network quality information: Include organization characteristics in the list of Wi-Fi organizations that are available, such as speed and sound quality.
- Allow for a persistent demand for information: Careful activities like games and video calls should be assigned an organizing need.
- Locate networks that seem dubious: Receive alerts when someone uses a live Wi-Fi network without authorization.
- Wi-Fi power-saving mode: To reduce power consumption, enable Wi-Fi traffic analysis. • Auto Hotspot connection: This feature automatically connects to a Wi-Fi area of interest upon recognition.
- Intelligent Wi-Fi: Examine the user-friendly version of this invention.

Advanced Wi-Fi Designs
You may manage stored organizations, check your device's organization address, and interact with various Wi-Fi networks

and hotspots. Expert cooperatives may provide a range of options.

1. Navigate to 📶 Connections > Wi-Fi in the Settings menu and tap ⬤ to activate Wi-Fi.

2. To see the related options, choose ⋮ More options > Advanced settings:

- o Samsung record and cloud adjustment: Samsung accounts and Wi-Fi profiles have to be in harmony.

- o Show Wi-Fi spring up: When I launch an application, let me know when Wi-Fi is available.

- o Wi-Fi and organization alarms: Locate organizations that are available within your area and get notifications when they are located.

- o Manage networks: See the networks that have been stored and decide which ones to delete or rejoin to next.

- Wi-Fi on/off history: View the apps that have recently enabled or disabled your Wi-Fi.
- Area of interest 2.0: Associate with WiFi networks that assist Area of interest 2.0 accordingly.
- Introduce network endorsements: Introduce confirmation statements.

Bluetooth

You may coordinate your device with other Bluetooth-empowered gadgets, including Bluetooth earbuds or in-vehicle theater systems. When a matching has been created, the gadgets may recall one another and transfer information without anticipating to input the passkey once more.

1. From the Settings menu, choose Connections > Bluetooth, then press to implement Bluetooth.
2. Tap a gadget and follow the instructions to lay out a relationship.

💡 Idea: Tap ✱ Bluetooth to use to this feature when sharing a file.

Rename the related gadget.
You may rename a connected device to make it easier to recognize.

1. Tap 📶 Connections > Bluetooth from the Settings menu. Then, press ⬭ to make Bluetooth pop on.

2. chose ⚙️ Settings by touching it, and thereafter chose Rename.

3. In the aftermath of checking the new name out, hit Rename.

Turn off from a Bluetooth item.
At the point when you unpair one Bluetooth gadget from another, the other will never again perceive the first, and you should coordinate with it again to rejoin.

1. From the Settings menu, choose 📶 Connections > Bluetooth, then touch to begin Bluetooth.

2. Pick ⚙️ Settings close to the device, and then Unpair.

3. Tap Unpair just to ensure.

Advanced Bluetooth settings

The High level menu adds enhanced Bluetooth accents. Various possibilities might be given by professional companies.

1. Pick Bluetooth under 🛜 Connections in the Settings menu.

2. Tap Progressed settings or ⋮ More options > High level settings to view the related decisions:

- Sync documents from the Samsung Cloud or your Samsung account that were transported using Bluetooth. Music Sharing: License companions to play music on your Bluetooth speaker or earbuds.

- Ringtone sync: Play the ringtone that is selected on a linked Bluetooth device when someone calls. Bluetooth control history: View the programs that have as of late used Bluetooth. Block pairing request : Add devices to hinder matching solicitations.

- Bluetooth scan history: Control an application's Bluetooth abilities and observe which programs have as of late sought for Bluetooth devices nearby.

Dual audio

Your device can play back sound to two paired Bluetooth sound gadgets.

1. Interface your telephone to sound devices that aid Bluetooth.
2. From the Warning board, pick the Media yield sign.

3. Tap ✅ the symbol near to every one of the two sound devices recorded under Sound result to begin playing sound.

NFC and Payment

You may chat with another gadget by means of Close to Handle Correspondence (NFC) without forming an organization affiliation. A couple of installation programs employ this method, for example, Android Shaft. As well as supporting NFC, the device you are transferring to should be situated four centimeters from your gadget.

o Go to Settings, choose 🛜 Connections > NFC and contactless installations, and then press ⬤ to enhance this alternative.

Utilize the tap and pay option.

Utilizing an NFC installment application, merely connect your portable to a feasible Visa peruser to begin making installments.

1. Pick Settings > 📶 Connections > NFC and contactless installations, then, at that point, touch ⬤ to begin NFC.

2. To access the default installment application, tap Contactless installments.

• To choose an alternative installment application, pick an application that is open.

• To use an open installment application, hit Pay using as of now open program.

• To make that help as the default, pick Others, then, at that point, your favorite installment plan.

Ultra-wideband

Learn the precise area of neighboring devices. Different alternatives might be given by expert groups.

Pick Settings > 📶 Connections > Ultra - wideband (UWB) to turn this functionality on.

Airplane mode

When the mobile phone is in solitary mode, all organization associations are off, including Bluetooth, Wi-Fi, portable information, calling, and informing. At the moment where Flight mode is dynamic, you may switch on Wi-Fi and Bluetooth in Settings or via the Fast Settings window.

o From the Settings menu, select 📶 Connections > Flight mode, then, at that point, press ⬭ to empower this decision.

💡 NOTE: Utilizing mobile phones on boats and aircraft could be dependent upon local, state, and federal restrictions and constraints. At the point when in quite mode, there will be no organization availability accessible. Incapacitating super wideband (UWB), which is forbidden on board ships and jets, should be feasible via flight mode. Continuously stick to team instructions in regards to when and how to use your gadget, and doubly verify with the proper professionals.

SIM organizer
Assuming your cell expert co-op and plan permit duplicate SIM (two genuine SIM cards), or eSIM (installed SIM), you may

possibly handle two flexible records without delivering two devices. Various possibilities might be given by expert co-ops.

Gadgets that support double SIM cards have two SIM card spaces. It might also contain a microSD card area for more capacity, if upheld. Programming upgrades for gadgets having multi SIM abilities will trigger the double SIM highlight put in after send off.

Gadgets that recognize an eSIM may be developed to such an extent that they can operate without the real SIM card inside them. This enables the utilization of the eSIM or traditional SIM card for texting, phone calls, and information. Programming updates for eSIM-fit mobile phones will actualize the included eSIM characteristics following send off.

○ From the Settings menu, choose Connections > SIM the board to view the related choices.

• SIM cards: You may view, utilize, rename, or deactivate the SIM cards that are truly introduced on your device.

• eSIMs: To add an arrangement from an outmoded gadget or to enroll for another eSIM flexible arrangement, press ╋ Add eSIM.

• Core SIM: While using a few SIM cards, allocate one vital SIM card to be used for information, messages, and calls.

• Extra SIM settings: Tap to examine and explore extra possibilities for managing SIM cards.

Mobilie networks

Utilize flexible organizations to arrange your gadget to join with and utilize portable organizations and portable information. Various possibilities might be given by professional companies.

○ From the Settings menu, click 📶 Connections > Versatile organizations.

• Versatile information: Give consent for its usage.

• Global information meandering: While visiting another country, adjust your choices for message, telephone, and information wandering.

• Information wandering access: Set up portable organization association while out and about. • Information meandering: Grant information utilization while on numerous flexible organizations.

• Upgraded Calling: To work with better communication, utilize LTE information.

• Framework select: Change the assistance provider's CDMA meandering mode, if suitable.

Pick or add Passage Names (APNs), which are the organization arrangements necessary for your gadget to link with your provider.

• Network heads: Pick networks that you need to use and can access to.

• Versatile organization diagnostics: Incorporate usage and analytic information for researching.

• Network extenders are cells that may increase the length of your organization association. Search out these.

TIP: Utilize these options to help you with adjusting association settings that can affect your month to month cost.

Data use

Check the information you are now utilizing on Wi-Fi and your telephone. Impediments and admonitions might also be modified.

○ From the Settings menu, choose Connections > Data usage.

Turn Data saver to ON.
Utilize Information Saver to reduce how much information you utilize by forestalling specified programs from transmitting or acquiring information behind the scenes.

1. From the Settings menu, click Connections > Information utilization > Information saver.

2. To begin Information Saver, tap .
• To provide particular programs unimpeded data usage while Information Saver is activated, pick Permitted to use information. You may likewise create particular lines by clicking the button near to each application.

Observe mobie information
You could rework your flexible information access by establishing specific limits and constraints. A range of choices

might be introduced by specialized groups.

○ From the Settings menu, choose Connections > Information usage. The options that are available are as follows: Utilize the portable information that is vital for your membership.

• Worldwide information meandering: Turn on portable information administrations while you're away from home.

• Portable simply applications: Set up your mobile phone to just employ flexible information, in any case, when it's linked with Wi-Fi.

• Versatile information utilization: Utilize portable associations with screen information usage over the long term. There is a display of both the general and application explicit usage.

• Information cautioning and charging cycle: Set the month to month date to match the day your expert organization enables charging.

TIP: Utilize these choices to watch out for your projected information utilization.

Monitor Wi-Fi data

You may restrict admission to Wi-Fi information by adjusting organizations and usage constraints.

1. Click the Settings menu and choose Connections > Data usage.

2. Tap Wi-Fi information usage to show information use after some time across Wi-Fi associations. There is a depiction of both the general and application explicit usage.

Mobile Hotspot

Versatile area of interest develops a Wi-Fi network that different gadgets may interface with by utilizing your information plan.

1. Select Connections > Mobile hotspot and tethering > Mobile hotspot from the Settings menu.

2. To activate the portable area of interest, tap ⬭.

3. Activate Wi-Fi on the devices you need to connect to, then choose your device's portable area of interest. To establish an association, enter the secret word for the portable area of interest.

• Under the "Associated gadgets" class, a list of related devices is shown.

Here's a hint: You can use your phone to scan a QR code to connect an additional device to your flexible area of interest without having to input a secret word.

Create the mobile hotspot settings.
You are in charge of the security and association settings for your flexible area of interest.

1. Select Connections > Versatile area of interest and tying > Portable area of interest from the Settings menu.
2. To change the options that follow, choose Design:
   • Network name: View and modify the name of the region that's handy for you.

   • Secret word: You may see or modify it, if you choose a security level that allows one.

   • Band: Choose a transfer speed from the available options.

• Security: Select the degree of protection appropriate for your broad topic of interest.

• Advanced: Create additional transportable areas of interest.

Auto hotspot

With various devices, you may share your interest affiliation when users enter into your Samsung account.

1. Select 📶 Connections > Versatile area of interest and tying > Portable area of interest from the Settings menu.

2. To activate the feature, tap ⬤ Auto hotspot.

Tethering

To share your device's Web association with another device, use tethering. A range of choices might be introduced by specialized groups.

1. Select 📶 Connections > Versatile area of interest and tying from the Settings menu.
2. Decide on a menu item:
   • Select Bluetooth tying to share the Web association on your device over Bluetooth.

• Choose USB tying after connecting the device and PC via a USB connection.

• Prior to enabling Ethernet tying, use an Ethernet connection to link the PC and device.

Look for devices in the area

Enabling Close by device scanning makes it easier to connect with other available devices. By using this feature, you will be notified when devices are available for association.

1. Select Connections > More association settings > Close by device scanning from the Settings menu.

2. To activate the component, tap .

Connect to a printer.

To print reports and images from your device, just connect it to a printer that is also linked to the same Wi-Fi network.

1. Select Connections > More connections options > Printing from the options menu.

2. Once you have selected "Default print administration," choose " ⋮ More choices > Add printer."

• In the unlikely event that your printer has to be downloaded, choose ✛ Download Module and follow the instructions to establish a print server.

☼ NOTE: Not every program has printing functionality.

Virtual Private Networks

Use a virtual private network, or VPN, to link your device to a secure, private network. The association details that your VPN executive provided are necessary.

1. Select 🛜 Connections > More Connection settings > VPN from the Settings menu.

2. Choose ⋮ More > Add VPN profile from the menu.

3. After entering the VPN network information that the executive in charge of your company has provided, click Save.

Manage VPN

To add or remove a VPN association, use the VPN settings option.

1. Select 📶 Connections > More connection settings > VPN from the Settings menu.

2. After selecting a VPN, tap ⚙️ Settings.
3. To make changes to the VPN, choose Save; to remove it, select Erase.

Create to VPN.

A VPN is easy to connect to and disconnect from once it is designed.

1. Select 📶 Connections > More connection settings > VPN from the Settings menu.
2. Choose a VPN, enter your login credentials, and then click Interface.

- Tap the VPN and then choose Separate to terminate the connection.

Private DNS

Your device may be designed to communicate with a private DNS server.

1. Select 📶 Connections > More connection settings > Confidential DNS from the Settings menu.
2. Select one of the options available to establish a private DNS association.
3. Press Save.

Ethernet

In the unlikely event that a distant organization association is not available, you may connect your device to a local organization via an Ethernet connection.

1. Attach your device to an Ethernet cable.

2. Choose ⬜Connections > More connection options > Ethernet from the options menu, then follow the on-screen instructions.

TIP: An Ethernet connection is anticipated to be interfaced with your device using a connector, which is not included.

Network lock status

Check whether your phone may be unlocked for usage on another flexible organization by seeing the organization lock status. Expert cooperatives may provide a range of options.

○ Select Associations > More connection settings > Networklock status from the Settings menu.

Joined devices

Make that your device can communicate via portable with other devices that are connected to it.

○ To see the related options, choose 🔲 Joined devices from the Settings menu:

➤ Quick Offer: Provide documents from your smartphone to anybody who have a Samsung account.

➤ Auto switch Buds: Whenever you play media, make a choice, or react to one, your System Buds will automatically transition from another device to this one.

➤ Message and approach various devices: Send and receive calls and messages using the Galaxy system devices that are linked to your Samsung account.

➤ Keep using apps on various devices: Pick up where you left off on System devices connected to your Samsung account.

➤ Windows Connection: Connect your device to a Windows computer to instantly access text messages, images, and other content.

➤ Multi-control: You may manipulate things and operate this gadget by pulling them to and fro using the console and cursor on your Universe Book.

➢ Samsung DeX: Connect your tablet to a computer or TV to enhance its ability to carry out different functions.

➢ Shrewd View: Play recordings on a nearby television or display the screen of your device.

➢ Universe Wearable: Connect your device to your Samsung earbuds and watch.

➢ SmartThings: Link your device to a network of resources for a smarter way of living.

➢ Android Auto: Connect your device to your car's display to help you focus on driving.

Vibrations and noises

You can adjust the noises and sensations that indicate screen interactions, alerts, and other activities.

Sound configuration

The device's sound mode may be changed without using the volume buttons.

○ Select a mode by selecting 🔊 Sounds and vibration in the Settings.

• Sound: Select the appropriate loudness, vibrations, and tones for alerts and messages.

- Vibrate as your device rings: Configure your device to both vibrate and ring when a call comes in.

• Vibrate: Keep vibration reserved for alerts and notifications.

• Silent: Turn off all of your phone's sounds.

    – One method of temporarily muting a device is to set a time restriction for it.

    –

TIP: To change the sound mode without losing your modified sound settings, use the sound mode option instead of the volume keys.

Making gestures
Turn the phone over or cover the screen to quickly reduce noise.

    ○ Select Quiet using signals under Movements and movements > Advanced highlights in the Settings menu.

Turn the light on.

You control how and when your smartphone vibrates.

1. Go to Settings and choose Vibration and Sounds.

177

2. To modify, tap the options:

• Look through pre-customized vibrating designs before making judgments.

• Take note of how vibration design is determined: Examine a variety of already tailored vibration designs.

• Vibration of the framework: Adjust the force of vibration and criticism as necessary.

- Framework vibration force: To adjust the vibration intensity, use the slider.

- Contact connections: When objects are held or tapped on the route buttons, the screen will vibrate.

- Dialing keypad: The keypad vibrates as you enter digits.

- Samsung console: The Samsung console vibrates as you write.

- Charging: A charger vibrates when it is plugged in.

- Shake while moving as a route indicator.

- Shake to adjust focus, switch to a different shooting mode, and use other camera functions.

• Vibration power: Adjust the vibration levels for calls, notifications, and contact commitment by dragging the sliders.

Volume

Adjust the volume of call ringtones, notifications, media, and system noises.

Make sure you choose 🔊Sounds and vibration > Volume from the Settings menu. At that point, adjust the sliders to accommodate all different kinds of sounds.

TIP: You may use the Volume keys to adjust the volume. When the button is pressed, a pop-up menu displaying the current sound kind and volume level appears. After pressing to expand the menu, you may adjust the level of the various sound types by dragging the sliders.

Press and hold the volume keys when watching media.
Instead of using the by and by selected sound sort, set the default activity of the Volume keys to control the media sound volume.

1. You'll see the Settings menu appear. Choose 🔊 Vibration and Sounds > Volume.

2. To make this option more powerful, tap Use Volume keys for media.

The maximum level of media volume
In order to prevent frustrations, make sure the device is operating at its maximum volume output when using Bluetooth speakers or headphones (which are not included).

1. You'll see the Settings menu appear. Choose 🔊 Vibration and Sounds > Volume.

2. Select Media volume limit under More settings.

3. To make this element dynamic, tap ⬤ .

    • Drag the Custom volume limit slider to adjust the loudest possible outcome.

    • In the unlikely event that you want to adjust the volume setting so that a PIN is required, choose Set volume limit PIN.

Ring tones

Personalize your call ringtone by choosing from a variety of pre-uttered sounds or by adding your own. A range of choices might be introduced by specialized groups.

1. You can choose 🔊 Sounds and vibration > Ringtone from the Settings menu.

2. To adjust the volume of the ringtone, drag the slider.

3. To set a sound recording as your ringtone, click ➕ Add; if not, tap a ringtone to hear an example and choose it.

Alert tone

Choose it if you want a single default sound for all notifications.

1. Select 🔊Sounds and vibration > Notice sound from the Settings menu.

2. To adjust the volume of the notice sound, drag the slider.

3. To hear a glimpse, select a sound by tapping it.

☼ Advice: You can also use the Application Settings board to customize the notification sounds for each application.

System Sound

You can adjust the sounds your device produces for various functions, like screen tapping and charging. Expert cooperatives may provide a range of options.

○ To view the related options, select 🔊 Sounds and vibration > Framework sound from the Settings menu:

o Framework sound volume: Adjust the clamor of the framework by dragging the slider.

o Framework sound subject: Select a sound topic for each highlight, such as Samsung console, charging, and contact cooperations.

o Contact associations: When you touch or tap the screen to select an option, sounds will start to play.

o Dialing keypad: Play a tone as you enter a number on the Telephone keypad.

o Samsung console: When using the Samsung console, make noises.

○ Charging: When a charger is plugged in, a sound will be made.

○ Lock and open the screen: When the screen is locked or opened, a sound will be heard.

Dolby Atmos

Take advantage of the Dolby Atmos quality when you play content that has been specially mixed for Atmos. This component is only helpful when a headset is connected.

○ To view the related choices, select Sounds and vibration > Sound quality and impacts from the Settings menu.

- Dolby Atmos: Lose yourself in cutting-edge surround and overhead sound.
- Switch to DTS-Atmos for computer games as Dolby Atmos isn't working properly right now.

Equalizer

You have the option to select a sound preset tailored to particular melodic types or manually adjust the sound settings.

1. Select 🔊 Sounds and vibration > Sound quality and impacts from the Settings menu.
2. Select the melodic kind by clicking the Balancer button.

UHQ upscaler

Improved sound quality is necessary for movies and music to be more easily audible. This part can only be accessed when a headset is connected.

1. Select 🔊 Sounds and vibration > Sound quality and impacts from the Settings menu.
2. Select an upscaling option by tapping UHQ upscaler.

Modify the audio

Optimize the audio quality for each ear to enhance your auditory pleasure.

1. Select 🔊 Sounds and vibration > Sound quality and impacts > Change sound from the Settings menu.
2. To select when to adjust the sound settings, tap Adjust sound.
3. You can adjust the sound profile by tapping on your #1 sound profile and selecting ⚙️Settings.

Counsel: To help your device determine which sound is most comfortable for you, please press If it's not too much trouble, test my hearing.

Separate app sound

On a Bluetooth speaker or headset, you can configure an application to play only media audio and to muffle all other sounds, including alerts. This option won't show up in the Sound gadget menu unless you're linked to a Bluetooth device.

1. From the Settings menu, choose Sounds and vibration > Separate application sound.

2. To play the Different application's sound, click Turn on quickly. Adjust the following setups after that:

  o Application: Select an application to stream audio to a different audio device.

  o Sound gadget: Select the device that will be used to play the sound for the application.

Notifications

You can refine and enhance application notifications by modifying which apps alert you and how they do so.

App alerts

You have the option to select which apps have ready features.

○ Select Notifications > Application warnings from the Settings menu. At that point, tap to enable explicit application warnings.

Alerts on the lock screen

You can choose which alerts appear on the lock screen.

○ Select Notification > Lock screen notifications from the Settings menu, then tap to activate the feature. Selecting a moveable option displays your selection:

o Content stowing away: Notices on the Notice board that kill moods.
o Current topic: Display notifications on the notice board.
o Display content when opened: When the screen is opened, display notice content.
o Warning display: Select which alerts to display on the Lock screen.

o Show on Consistently In Plain View: Enable the Consistently In Plain View screen to view warnings.

Notifications Pop-up style

You have the ability to modify various settings and the style of your notices.

○ Press Notifications > Notice spring up style to choose a warning spring up style from the Settings menu.

o Compact: Permit you to reissue your alerts.

o Apps to display briefly: Select which applications to display as urgent warnings.

o Edge lighting style: Use the edge lighting plan for warnings.

o Variety by catchphrase: Select distinctive tones for alerts that contain keywords you think are really important.

o Show even when show is off: Select whether to display images when the screen is lowered in any situation.

o Step-by-step: To start, open the Samsung Notice settings.

Do not disturb

It is possible to disable alerts and sounds when in the "don't upset" setting. Additionally, you have the option to create exceptions for specific users, programs, and warnings. It is also possible to schedule regular tasks such as getting together and sleeping.

○ Choose notifications> Don't upset from the Settings menu. Next, create the coordinating:

o Try not to get upset: Make use of this ability to silence rumblings and alerts.
o How much time will it take? When you physically enter the Don't Upset mode, you have the option to select a preset span.
o Arrange
o Rest: Create a revised rest schedule that incorporates a "don't upset" clause.
o Create a schedule: Schedule the days and times that you will regularly put your device in "don't upset" mode to create another daily routine.

Allowed throughout Do not disturb

➢ Messages and calls: Snap to activate the special Don't Upset cases.

> Application warnings: Include the apps that you want alerts from in "Don't upset" mode. Talk, message, and call warnings will continue to be sent to you even if you block access to the relevant applications.

> Alerts and sounds: When the don't disturb mode is dynamic, activate alerts, vibrations, and occasions.

> Hide alerts: To hide notifications, navigate to the customization settings.

Advanced notifications setups

Notifications that you receive from applications and services can be changed.

○ Select 📷 Notifications > High level settings from the Settings menu.

> Notice symbol show: Modify the quantity of alerts displayed in the Status bar.

> Display battery rate: The Status bar on your phone will indicate how long its battery lasts on average.

> Take note of history: Display most recent, few, and paused alarms.

> Conversations: See the cautions associated with the conversations. Make contact and have a conversation

about warnings in order to calm, caution, or necessitate them.

➢ Drifting notices: Choose Savvy spring up view or Air pockets to activate drifting alerts.

➢ Reactions to notice ideas: Obtain practical guidance on the appropriate course of action in response to alerts and warnings.

➢ Show nap button: Make a button appear so you can quickly turn off notifications.

➢ Updates for warnings: Configure and alter recurring alerts for notifications from specific programs and services. Delete the notices to mitigate the warnings.

➢ Application symbol identifications: By looking at the identifications that appear on your applications' symbols, you can determine which of your applications are currently receiving warnings. It is anticipated that tapping will alternate between identifications that show the number of uninitiated warnings.

➢ Remote Crisis Alerts: Customize alerts for emergencies to suit your preferences.

Take note when you pick up the phone.
When you first get your phone, in order to enable vibration alerts for missed calls and messages,

Go to Settings > High level components > Motions and gestures > Alert when phone picked up to enable.

Display
Along with many other showcase settings, you can alter the text size, break delay, and screen brightness.

Dim mode
During the evening, you can switch to a less visible topic by utilizing the dim mode, which lessens the brightness of bright or white screens and notifications.

○ To view these options, select Display from the Settings menu:
- Light: Set your phone's default theme to something light-colored.
- Dark: Choose a low-light variety theme for your device.

Designs for the dim mode: The dim mode's application is flexible in terms of timing and location.

- Turn on time: Switch from the dim mode to a personalized schedule or from dusk to dawn.

Screen brightness

The brightness of the screen can be adjusted to suit specific lighting conditions or personal preferences.

1. Navigate to Settings and select Display from there.
2. Change the levels of brilliance:

• To adjust the splendor level, use the Brilliance slider.

• To have the screen automatically adjust its brightness based on the available light, tap Versatile Splendor. Choose Extra splendor to increase the splendor to its highest degree

– If Versatile brilliance is not selected. With this, more batteries are used.

Counsel: In addition, you can adjust the screen's brightness using the Fast Settings box.

Motion smoothness

With a higher rate of energy, the lookover will be more fluid and the liveliness more sensible.

1. Select Display> Movement perfection from the Settings menu.
2. Once you've selected an option, click Apply.

Eye care

This component may improve your sleep and reduce eye strain. Organizing the programmed on and off of this capability is possible.

1. Select Display> Eye Solace Protection from the Settings menu, then tap to activate this feature.
2. Select a decision to change:

   • Adaptable: This feature automatically modifies the color temperature of your screen based on how you use it and the time of day.

   • Customize the timetable to your preferences to determine when to activate the Eye Solace Safeguard.

   > -By pressing Set plan, you can choose Consistently on, Nightfall to Dawn, or Custom.

- Adjust the channel's haziness by using the Variety temperature slider.

• A more noticeable simplicity in altering the showcase's variety tones and differences for a happier review insight.

Screen Performance

You can adjust the screen quality for different situations using the different screen mode settings on your device. The mode can be adjusted to suit your preferences.

1. Screen mode is selectable in the Settings menu under ⚙ Display.

2. Select a button to switch the screen's orientation.

To adjust the white equilibrium, use the slider.

If you want to alter the RGB values physically, tap Progressed settings.

Text size and style

To customize your device, you can alter the text style and size.

○ To view the related options, select ⚙ Display > Font dimension and style from the Settings menu:

194

To modify the text style, tap the typeface style.

Select it, agitate the town; alternatively, click ✛ Download text styles to add text styles from the Universe Store.

To give all textual styles a strong weight, choose the Intense typeface.

To adjust the text's size, drag the Text dimension slider.

Enlarge Image
To make the substance easier to see, adjust the zoom level.

1. In the Settings menu, tap ⚙ Display, then select Zoom the screen while in plain view.
2. To adjust the zoom level, drag the zoom slider on the screen.

Screen resolution
On the WorldS24 Ultra, you can adjust the screen goal to sharpen the image or lower it to conserve battery life.

1. Select the ⚙ Display> Screen resolution option from the Settings menu.

2. After selecting your preferred objective, click Apply.

-☼- REMEMBER: Certain programs could really shut and not recognize changes to the screen objective.

Apps on display in full screen
In the end, it comes down to choose which apps to run in the percentage of the whole screen angle.

○ To enable and modify this feature, choose ⚙ Display > Full screen apps from the Settings menu. Then, touch the programs to adjust their settings.

Camera cutout
It is possible to hide the camera pattern area with a dark strip.

○ To activate and modify this aspect, choose ⚙Display> Camera pattern from the Settings menu. Afterwards, hit applications.

Screen timeout
The screen may be set to turn off after a certain amount of time.

○ To set a time limit, choose ⚙ Display> Screen break from the Settings menu and press it.

💡 Keep in mind that using still photos over longer periods of time may result in persistent afterimages that resemble ghosts or deteriorated image quality. When the presentation screen is no longer in use, turn it off.

Touch protection

When the device is in a dimly light area, such a pocket or backpack, the touch sensitivity of the screen is compromised.

   o   To activate the element, choose ⚙ Display > Coincidental touch protection from the Settings menu.

Touch awareness

Enhance the touch sensitivity of the screen while using screen protectors.

○ To activate it, choose ⚙ Display> Contact aversion from the Settings menu.

Display charging information

When the screen is off, the battery level and estimated time till the device is fully charged may be shown.

• To activate, choose ⚙ Display > Show charging statistics from the Settings menu.

Screen saver

You may choose to see images or other content while the screen dims or charges.
1. You'll see the Settings menu appear. Choose Screen Saver under ⚙ Display.
2. Select one of the options already illustrated:

- None: The screen saver that kills your mood.
- Colors: To see a tone-changing panel, tap the selection.
- picture table: Use a picture table to display your photos.
- Photo positioning: To hold photographs, use a photo placement.
- Photos: Display photos from your collection on Google Photos.

4. To see an example of the selected screen saver, tap See.

Advice: To access more options, tap the ⚙ options button.

Raise to wake

o To activate the screen, raise the device.

To activate this component, go to Settings > ⊕ High level elements > Movements and movements > Lift to wake.

To turn on the screen, double tap.

You may double tap the screen to turn it on instead than using the Side key.

o Select ⊕ Progressed highlights > Movements and movements > from the Settings menu. Tapping the screen twice will enable this feature.

To turn off the screen, double tap

Double tapping turns off the screen, unlike using the Side key.

o Select ⊕ Progressed highlights > Movements and movements > from the Settings menu. Tapping the screen twice will activate this feature and deactivate it.

Continue to watch with the screen on.
To keep it on, use the front camera to detect when you are looking at the screen.

○ Select ✪ Progressed highlights > Movements and signals > from the Settings menu. As you watch, keep the screen on and touch ⬤▷ to make use of the feature.

Single-hand mode
You may customize the screen layout to enhance your phone's one-handed use.

1. Select ✪ "Progressed highlights > One-gave mode" from the Settings menu.
2. After tapping ⬤▷ to activate the part, choose one of the following selections:
   • Motion: Press and hold the bottom border of the screen's focus point.
   • Button: To reduce the size of the presentation, press and hold the Home button ⬜ twice right away.

Security and lock screen
You may acquire your phone and set a screen lock to protect your info.

Different kinds of screen locks

The screen lock kinds that come with them are None, PIN, Example, Swipe, and Secret key; they provide no, medium, or high security.

Note: You may also use biometric locks to protect sensitive information on your device and prevent unauthorized access.

Install a security screen lock.
It is advised that you employ a secure screen lock (secret word, PIN, etc.) in order to access your mobile phone. This is necessary to set up and activate biometric locks.

1. You may choose a solid screen lock (Example, PIN, or Secret phrase) by selecting 🔒 Lock screen > Screen lock type from the Settings menu.
2. To display cautions on the lock screen, press ⬭. The options that are available are as follows:
   • Hiding Information: Avoid posting notifications on the notice board.
   • Current topic: Display notifications on the notice board.

• Display content when opened: When the screen is opened, display notice content.

• Notice display: Select which alerts to display on the Lock screen.

• Display on Consistently In Plain display: Activate the Consistently In Plain View screen to display alerts.

3. To dismiss the menu, tap Done.

4. Modify the corresponding screen lock configurations:

Shrewd Lock: This feature unlocks your device when it senses that certain regionsor other devices are unguarded. For this component, a secured screen lock is essential.

Secure lock settings: Modify the settings on your safe lock. For this element, a secured screen lock is necessary.

Lock screen: You may modify what shows on the lock screen by tapping.

Gadgets: Tap to switch between the devices that appear next to the clock on the Lock screen.

Contact and hold altering: Select whether to allow you to make changes with your finger on the Lock screen.

Constantly in plain sight: Ensure that the screen is always on.

Wandering clock: When you're out and about, display the time wherever you are.

About lock screen: Update the product for the lock screen.

Locate My Phone

By enabling remote information deletion, internet tracking, and highlight locking, you may protect your device from theft or bad luck. To use See as My Portable, you must have a Samsung account and have Google area administration enabled.

Activate "Track down My Telephone."
The Find My Versatile feature has to be launched and adjusted before using it. For remote access to your phone, go to findmymobile.samsung.com.

1. Select Security and protection > See as My Versatile > Allow this phone to be located from the Settings menu.
2. To enable View as My Portable and come near enough to your Samsung account, tap . The options that are available are as follows:
  – Allow this phone to be located: You may enable this feature to

help locate this device by turning it on.

- Remote open: Give Samsung permission to save your PIN, secret key, or other key so you may access and manage your phone from a secure location.
- Transmit last area: When your device's battery life starts to dwindle, let it to transmit its last area to the Find My Versatile server.

Play Safe from Google

You may choose to have Google Play scan your device and its apps for viruses and other security risks.

○ Select Google Play Safeguard under ⬤Security and security > Application security from the Settings menu.

• Programed confirmation is applied to refreshes.

Updates regarding security

Finding out when the security programming was last updated and if any more recent forms are available may be done easily.

○ To see the most current security update released and verify if a more recent version is available, go to Settings > ⬤Security and protection > Updates > Security form.

Permission manager

In any case, an application may still be able to access device features like the camera, amplifier, or area even while it is closed and operating in the background. You may choose to get notifications from your device anytime anything occurs.

1. From the Settings menu, choose ⬤ Security and protection > Security > Consent supervisor.

2. To choose which consents you want to learn more about, choose a classification and then an application first.

Note: Upon launching an application or engaging with an intriguing feature, you will be presented with an exchange box asking for permission to use certain features on your device.

Controls and alerts

Restrict which apps have access to the microphone, camera, and clipboard.

1. Choose Protection under ⬤Security and privacy from the Settings menu.

2. Turn the corresponding options to strengthen or weaken the controls and warnings:

 • Camera access: Provide applications with the necessary authorization to get access to the camera.

 • Amplifier access: Give apps the appropriate permission to access the mouthpiece.

 • Receive notifications when an application copies material to the clipboard.

Samsung Privacy

Provide Samsung analytical data, supposing that specific problems are occurring with your device.

1. Select ⬤Security and protection > Protection > Other protection selections from the options menu.

2. To make adjustments, choose the corresponding options under Samsung:

- Samsung Security: Access information on Samsung's security measures.
- Customization Administration: Permit Samsung to provide you with information and suggestions based on your preferences.
- Send demonstrative data: In the unlikely event that your device isn't operating as intended, send Samsung analytical data.

Google's Information Security

Adjust the Google and Android security settings.

1. Select ⬤ Security and protection > Security > Other protection choices from the options menu.
2. Tap to modify Google's security settings.

Samsung Pass

Use Samsung Pass to get biometric information access to your top services. To use Samsung Pass, you must log into your Samsung account.

1.Select ⬤ Security and protection > Samsung Pass from the Settings menu.
2. After logging into your Samsung account, provide your biometric data.

Secured Safe

On your phone, you may create a secure organizer to keep confidential information and unfinished tasks out of the hands of nosy groups. For the purpose of setting up and using Secure envelope, you must log into your Samsung account.

- o To get content on your phone, go to Settings > Security and protection > Secure Envelope. Then, follow the on-screen instructions.

Secure Wi-Fi

Whenever you use public Wi-Fi networks, be sure you have extra security protection. In order to activate and configure Secure Wi-Fi, you should truly log into your Samsung account.

- o Select Security and protection > from the Settings menu. To get protection guarantee, make sure your Wi-Fi is secure and follow the setup instructions.

Personal Communication

You may choose expiration dates, distribute documents anonymously, and prevent recipients from sharing them again. Information insurance benefits from blockchain innovation.

○ Select Settings > ⬤ Security and protection > Confidential sharing, then adhere to the on-screen instructions to add records.

Blockchain Keystore from Samsung

Maintain the confidentiality of your blockchain private key. Expert cooperatives may provide a range of options.

1. Select ⬤ Security and protection > Samsung Blockchain Keystore from the Settings menu.
2. To import or create a new bitcoin wallet, follow the bearings.

Install unknown apps

You may provide permission to introduce cryptic third-party projects from certain websites or apps.

1. From the Settings menu, choose ⬤ Security and protection >. Present esoteric uses.

2. Tap ⬤ to support the creation of an application or source.

TIP: Installing unknown third-party apps may increase the vulnerability of your device and personal data to security threats.

Factory data reset password

To return your phone to its factory settings, you may need to know the secret phrase. A range of choices might be introduced by specialized groups.

○ Choose 🔵 Security and protection > Additional security options > Click the settings menu, input a secret key, and then configure or modify the passphrase.

Configure your SIM card lock.

You may use a PIN to lock your SIM card so that unauthorized users cannot use it in another device. A range of choices might be introduced by specialized groups.

    ○ Select 🔵 Security and protection > Other security choices > from the menu of options. Establish the SIM card lock and adhere to the guidelines.

        • To activate the element, just tap the Lock SIM card.

- To create a new PIN, choose Change SIM card PIN.

View passwords

You have the option to have characters appear as you enter in secret key fields.

  o Select ⬤ Security and protection > Other security choices > from the menu of options. Passwords need to be sent in order to activate this feature.

Device Organization

You may provide managers access to programs and security features on your mobile device.

1. Select ⬤ Security and protection > Other security options > Gadget administrator apps from the settings menu.
2. To enable the device, click the executive mode option.

Credentials maintenance

Reasonably believed security declarations are loaded into your device and verify the authenticity of servers for safe relationships.

○ To see the related options, choose Security and protection > Other security settings from the Settings menu:

   • Examine security certifications: Display the certificates on the back of your device. Examine the customer statements linked to your device.

   • Introduce right out of capacity: Use the phone's or device's capacity to introduce an additional authentication.

   • Clear certifications: Reset the secret word and remove the objects in the qualification from the device.

   • Declaration of the board application: To see the things in your qualifications, choose an executive confirmation application.

Advanced security protocols

With the help of these options, you may adjust your device's high level security settings to better protect it.

○ To see the related options, choose Security and protection > Other security settings from the Settings menu:

• Trust specialists: Authorize linked, trusted devices to do certain tasks. This option only appears when the lock screen is activated. Application pin: When an application is fixed to the screen, you are unable to use other features of your device.

• Update the Universe foundation application: Create your smartphone to accommodate future Samsung updates.

• Security strategy updates: Make sure to regularly check for updates to ensure your device is secure.

Location

Wi-Fi, GPS, and portable organizations are all used by area administrations to determine the precise location of your device.

1. Choose Location from the Settings menu.

2. To initiate area administrations, tap .

Concept: For some applications to function, area administrations need have more authority.

Permission for applications

The authorizations for any apps that need access to your local information should be properly established.

1. You may choose Location > Application authorizations from the Settings menu.

2. Select which area freedoms to assign to an application by tapping on it. Every application provides unique options for layout.

Location Services

The most recent location data is saved and used by area governments on your device. Some apps may use this data to enhance your search results by taking your visited locations into account.

1. Choose Location from the Settings menu.

2. To see how your region information is used, choose a section under region administrations.

Improved accuracy

Implement further area-examining programming.

1. Location > Area administrations may be selected from the Settings menu.

2. Click on an association option under Lift accuracy to add or remove area administrations:

• Wi-Fi checking: Give programs and services permission to automatically look for Wi-Fi networks, even while the company is not in use.

• Bluetooth checking: Give apps permission to use Bluetooth to automatically locate and connect to nearby devices, even when Bluetooth is turned off.

Most recent accessibility

See a summary of all the apps that have made reference to a certain location.

1. Choose Area from the Settings menu.

2. To initiate area administrations, tap .

3. To access the settings of the application, tap anything under "Ongoing admittance."

Emergency Location Service

At the point when you SMS or contact a crisis number, your gadget might promptly convey its location to crisis response accomplices in the event that your region sustains Crisis location Administration (ELS).

1. From the Settings menu, click Security and crises > crisis Area Administration.
2. To switch on Crisis Area Help, press .

Accounts
You approach and command over your records, which integrate Google and Samsung records, email, and virtual entertainment.

Add an account
You could add and synchronize all of your informal conversation, email, and photo and video sharing records.

1. From the Settings menu, choose Records and reinforcement > Oversee accounts > Add account.
2. Click on a certain record type.

3. Follow the steps to set up the record and input your login info.

- To enable scheduled account refreshes, choose the option entitled "Auto sync information."

Account settings

Each record has obvious tendencies. For all records of similar sort, regular settings may be created. The accessible parts and record settings alter dependent upon the kind of record.

1. From the Settings menu, choose Records and reinforcement > Oversee accounts.

2. To modify a record's inclinations, touch it.

Take out an account

You may delete accounts from your device.

1. From the Settings menu, choose Records and reinforcement > Oversee accounts.

2. In the aftermath of compressing the record, choose Eliminate account.

Back up, then use it to restore

You may arrange your device to preserve information supplements to particular records.

Samsung account

It is achievable to enable information reinforcements to your Samsung account. Expert cooperatives may provide a range of options.

○ From the Settings menu, choose 🔄 Records and Reinforcement. Then, pick a Samsung Cloud choice:
- Make an information reinforcement by putting up your Samsung record to do as such.
- Reestablish information: Sign into your Samsung record to go to your reinforcement information.

Login with Google
Allowing information reinforcements to your Google Record is a decision.

1. Under Settings, choose 🔄Records and reinforcement.
2. Select Google Drive information reinforcement.

External storage move

You may either use Brilliant Change to reestablish the reinforcement information or reinforcement the information to a USB storage gadget.

○ From the Settings menu, choose ⟳ Records and reinforcement > Outside capacity move.

Google settings

You may adjust the Google settings on your mobile phone. Your Google Record works out which alternatives are available.

○ Select an adjustable option in the wake of selecting Ⓖ Google from the Settings menu.

Device maintenance

View the condition with your gadget's battery, stockpiling, and memory. You might likewise configure your gadget to subsequently boost its structure assets.

Fast enhancement

The rapid enhancement highlight accomplishes the accompanying actions to further expand gadget execution:

• Finding and wiping off apps that use an abnormal measure of battery duration.

• Taking out unessential scraping and shutting down foundation running apps.

• Malware identification

From the Settings menu, select ⚙ Battery and gadget care > Advance swiftly to enable the fast streamlining highlight.

Battery

Look at the many approaches by which your gadget consumes the battery.

○ Pick Settings > Battery and gadget maintenance > ⚙ Battery to examine the accompanying selections.

• Power saving: To widen battery lifetime, restrict foundation area checks, matching up, and network use. You might choose other power-saving judgments to conserve significantly more energy when this mode is activated.

• Limitations on foundation usage: View infrequently used programs and restrict battery use edges to them. To degrade this part, just pick Set away any unnecessary tasks.

• Use since previous full charge: Perceive how much battery you've as of late used by administration, application, and time.

• Remote power sharing: To enable feasible devices to charge remotely, employ the battery on your gadget.

• Extra battery settings: Arrange alarms and extra battery qualities.

Storage

View the particulars of your stockpile usage and restrict by document type and categorization.

○ From the Settings menu, choose Battery and gadget maintenance > Capacity.

• To see and manage documents, choose a category.

Memory

Examine the available memory. To speed up your device, you may reduce the amount of Slam you use and shut foundation programs.

○ Select Battery and gadget maintenance > Memory from the Settings menu. Both spent and free smash are shown.

- In order to simplify Slam, click Clean now.

- To see the whole list of managers and apps that are using RAM, choose see more, Get more. You may tap ✓ to add or remove these services and programs.

- To see the apps and services that are included in this category, tap the applications that you haven't used recently. You may tap ✓ to add or remove these services and programs.

- To see a list of apps that have been blocked, tap Prohibited applications. To choose which apps to avoid based on memory utilization reviews, tap + Add Apps.

- Tap Slam To enhance application performance, you may also choose the amount of internal storage that will be used as virtual memory.

Choices for sophisticated device maintenance

Additional device support features may be accessed via the Advanced menu. Every specialized organization has a remarkable decision-making process.

- Select 🔘 "Battery and gadget care" from the Settings menu. The options that are available are as follows:

- Search: Locate boards that can be presented or that have been introduced in the past.

- Care report: Learn about temperature and charging guidelines, as well as the background information on restarts.

Alternative options:

Display the Applications screen with the Gadget Care icon. - Display the Applications window.

Contact us: Use Samsung individuals to get in touch with Samsung support.

Concerning maintaining your device: Examine the version and provide access to the Gadget Care information.

• Auto streamlining: To ensure maximum execution, restart organically on a case-by-case basis.

• Programming update: Verify if your software has been updated.

• Diagnostics: Check the condition of various components, charging, sensors, and touch screen.

• Maintenance mode: Enable your phone to protect you while it's being mended or used by someone else.

Language and Input

Choose the information and language on your device.

Modify the device's language

Dialects may be added to your roster and organized in any way you like. In the unlikely event that a program is unable to function in the language you have selected, it will switch to the next supported language in your list.

1. Select Language under ⬤ Broad administration from the Settings menu.

2. To choose a language from the list, tap ➕ Add language.

3. To modify the language of the gadget, tap Set as default.

- Select Apply after tapping a different language from the drop-down menu to make your selection.

App languages

Choose the language that each software uses by default.

1. Select ⬛ General administration > Application dialects from the Settings menu.

2. To switch the language by default, tap a program.

Text-to-speech

Create your text-to-discourse (TTS) preferences. Voice Assistant is one of the several TTS-based openness solutions.

○ To access the options, go to Settings > ⬛ General administration > Text-to-discourse.

- Best motor: Review Google's and Samsung's text-to-discourse motors. Click ⚙ Settings to display options.

• Language: Decide the language you like to use for communication.

• Discourse rate: Regulate the speaking tempo of the text.

• Pitch: Modify the discourse's pitch.

• Play: Snap to launch a brief conversation blend demonstration.

• Reset: Modify the cadence and pitch of your speech.

Change voice input language.

Obtain language packs so you may use them offline.

1. Choose ⚙General administration > Voice input from the Settings menu.

2. Select a language pack in order to use voice input while not connected.

Rundown of console keys and default

Console settings, built-in consoles, and default consoles may all be altered.

○ Select ⚙General administration > Console list from the Settings menu. Next, configure the default parameters that go with it:

• Default console: Select the console that automatically shows up on your device as you navigate menus and consoles.

• Samsung console: Modify the console's borders.

• Google Voice Composing: Modify Google Voice's information preferences.

• Console button on route bar: You can quickly switch between consoles by activating a button on the menu bar.

Physical consoles/Keyboard

By connecting a physical keyboard (separately available), you may alter the settings that are accessible on your phone.

1. Click Settings and choose ⬛General administration.

2. Tap on physical keyboard, select:

• Display console on screen: Display the console on the screen while using a real console.

• Console simple routes: Display a screen representation of each console easy route.

• Modify language in a different way: On your real console, you may enable or disable language key shortcuts.

Trackpad and mouse
Create the button assignments and pointer speed for a trackpad or extra mouse (not included).

○ Select General administration > Mouse and trackpad from the Settings menu.

• Pointer speed: To adjust the pointer's speed, drag the slider to the left or right.

• Drag the slider to the left or right to adjust the wheel's scrolling speed. The wheel will scroll faster or slower depending on the setting.

• Increment pointer precision: Depending on the mouse development speed, the mouse cursor's speed may be adjusted.

• Pointer size and variety: Modify the mouse pointer's size and color.

• Essential mouse button: Select your essential mouse button by using either the Left or Right mouse button.

• Optional button: Select the mouse button's auxiliary function.

• Center button: Select the center button feature on the mouse.

• An additional button Select an activity by using an available mouse button.

• An additional button 2: Select a task for an additional, easily accessible mouse button.

Autofill and passwords

When inputting data, utilize autofill administrations to save time.

1. Select ⬚ General Administration under Settings.

2. After choosing Passwords and autofill, the selected administrations will appear.

Time and date

Of course, the wireless network sends date and time information to your device. The date and time may be altered manually whether or not you are not online.

○ Select ⬚ General administration > Date and time from the Settings menu.

The options that are accessible are as follows:

- Scheduled date and time: Get the most recent day and time information from your out-of-state company. When you turn off the scheduled date and time, you may choose from the options below:
  - Date set: Type the weekday in.
  - Set time: Type in the current duration.

- Programmed time region: Make use of the time zone that your portable provider specifies.
  - Choose a time zone: Make a different choice.

- Time region change dependent on area: Receive updates based on your present location.

- Make use of the 24-hour design: Choose the configuration for the time display.

Customization Service

Samsung products, services, and programming are designed to provide you with a personalized experience by skillfully anticipating your needs and goals. Samsung's Customization Administration uses the information it gathers about you and your use of its services to provide suggestions and personalized content to enhance your overall experience.

○ Select ⚌ General administration > Customization administration from the Settings menu.

Troubleshooting

On your device, you may check for programming upgrades and reset the administrations.

System/Software updates

If there are any available programming updates for your device, search for them and install them. Each assistance provider may provide a different option.

  o Choose   Programming update/Framework redesigns from the Settings menu to access the accompanying choices.

    • Check for refreshes: Conduct a manual search for programming refreshes.

- Programming update check: Physically inspect programming refreshes.
- Update us: Carrying out a previously postponed update
- Display previous programming refreshes: See a backdrop with all of the product refreshes done to your device.
- Shrewd adjustments: Install security updates consistently.
- Use the product overhaul tool and introduce a framework update establishment tool.

Start again from scratch.
Reset the device and system configurations. Resetting your device to its processing plant settings is an additional option.

Reset settings.
With the exception of the record, language, and security settings, your device's settings are unquestionably restored to their original plant settings. Private information is unaffected.

1. Select ⚙ General administration > Reset > Reset all settings from the Settings menu.

2. To reset the settings, click Reset; confirm when prompted.

Reset network configuration.
Wi-Fi, Bluetooth, and versatile information settings may all be cleared by using the reset network settings feature.

1. Select ⚙ General administration > Reset > Reset network settings from the Settings menu.
2. Select Reset settings; respond positively when prompted.

Reset accessibility settings.
It is possible to reset a device's openness settings. Both your personal information and the availability settings of downloaded applications remain unchanged.

1. From the Settings menu, choose ⚙ General administration > Reset > Reset openness settings.
2. To reset the settings, click Reset; confirm when prompted.

Factory Reset

By going back to the original settings, you may erase all of the data on your phone.

This permanently deletes all data from the device, including documents, music, images, videos, downloaded apps, framework and application data, Google or other record settings, and other information.

Constructing a lock screen on your device, when approved into a Google Record, automatically implements Google Gadget Security.

It should be noted that resetting a Google Record secret word may take a full day to show results on all devices linked to the record.

Prior to the device being reset:
1. Verify that the information you must maintain has been transferred to the capacity area.
2. Enter and confirm your Google Record login credentials.

Resetting your device:

1. Select ⚏ General administration > Reset > Processing plant information reset from the Settings menu.

2. To finish the reset, tap Reset and adhere to the instructions.

3. When it comes back, create your device according to the instructions for arrangement.

Google Device Security
Google mobile phone security is activated when you choose Lock screen after logging into a Google Record on your phone. This feature checks your personality using Google account data, protecting your phone against unintentional plant information resets.

Turn on the Google Device Shield.
Google mobile security starts to happen automatically when you set up a lock screen and add a Google Record to your phone.

Take down Google Device Guard.
You may either remove all Google Records from the device or the lock screen in order to disable Google Gadget Insurance.

Remove Google accounts using these steps:

1. From the Settings menu, choose ⟳ Records and reinforcement > Oversee accounts > [Google Account].
2. Select "Erase account."
Removing a secure lock screen:

1. Choose 🔒 Lock screen > Screen lock type from the Settings menu.
2. Select either Swipe or None.

Accessibility
There are options for availability for anybody who need help with seeing, hearing, or using their device in a different way. Thanks to exceptional features known as availability administrations, using a mobile phone has become easier for everyone.

Recommended for you
See a summary of the transparency features that you are currently using along with a list of recommended options that you may need to enable.

To see the suggestions, choose 👤 Accessibility > Prescribed from the Settings menu.

Talk-Back

Make advantage of certain settings and controls to browse without looking at the screen.

1. Navigate to TalkBack > Settings and choose Accessibility.

2. To bring up the functionality, press it first, then tap an option to adjust:

TalkBack Easy route: Select a different path to get TalkBack going fast.

Parameters: Set the TalkBack limits for more helpful assistance.

Verbal assistance

Use certain menu items and settings to browse without having to look at the screen.

1. Choose Spoken help under Accessibility from the Settings menu.

2. Press to activate the element, and then press a modification option:

- Read aloud from the console: The device can read, allowing others to hear the characters you write.

- Sound portrayal: When viewing recordings, if a sound soundtrack with a sound representation is available, it will be selected automatically.

- Perceivability of the Bixby Vision: Assign choices for loudly reading texts, illustrating scenery, identifying colors, and other functions.
- Voice Mark: By having voice accounts on NFC labels decoded, you may get information on certain goods or regions (excluded).
-

Visibility extensions

You may use features of accessibility to assist with your device's visual components.

Clarity and colour

To make the text and other elements of the screen easier to view, you may alter their contrast and variety.

○ Select Accessibility > Perceivability upgrades from the Settings menu, and then select one of the options below:

• Select the easily navigable showcase mode and click "Apply now":

> - Default: The show's default operation.
> - High differentiation: Lessen obscurity and straightforwardness, High differentiation text styles, High difference console, and Dim mode are all fully initiated.

> - Superb display: Text size, screen magnification, and the Striking and Feature buttons are fully functional.

• High difference subject: To make the screen easier to review, adjust the typeface and variety plan to increase contrast.

• High differentiation typefaces: Modify the arrangement and variety of a textual style to help it contrast more sharply with the background.

• High differentiation console: To improve the contrast between the keys and the foundation, you can modify the size and variety of the Samsung console.

• Cause to notice buttons: To make buttons stand out more against the background, use buttons with colored foundations.

• Change the text's hue so that it appears white on a dark background as opposed to dark on a white one.

• Variety remedy: If you have trouble seeing a particular tone, adjust the screen's tone.

• Variety channel: If you're having trouble reading the text, adjust the screen's tone.

• Remove the activities: Remove some of the screen impacts if you have a movement infection.

• Lessen clarity and obscurity: Reduce the amount of enhanced menu and exchange box visualizations to improve reading.

• Extra faint: For a more accessible to review insight, fade the screen past the lowest brilliance setting. Click to view more options.

Size and enlargement
On your device, you can create shortcuts for openness highlights and amplify functional screen elements.

○ Select 🧍Accessibility > Perceivability upgrades from the Settings menu, and then select one of the options below:
• Amplification: Use your fingertips to perform triple tapping, twofold squeezing, and hauling two fingers across the screen.

• Magnifier: Use the camera to enlarge the elements in your surroundings.

• Pointer size and variety: If your touchpad or mouse is connected, use a massive pointer (frill excluded).

• Text dimension and style: Arrange the presentation's text styles.

• Screen zoom: Adjust the level of magnification.

Hearing enhancements

You can adjust settings like hearing aid support, sound equilibrium, and similarity with listening devices to improve your collaboration with the device's audio.

  ○ Once you've navigated to Settings >
    Accessibility > Hearing
    enhancements, select this option:

      • Continuous messaging: Start RTT (continuous messaging) calls.

      • Live Translation: Record audio using a receiver, then translate it into text.

- Live Inscription: You can instantly transcribe expressed content from your device by using this feature.
- Close captioning and captioning inclinations: Provide services for these.
- Sound alerts: Receive alerts when a child cries or the doorbell rings.
- Support for amplifiers: To improve the functionality of your portable hearing aids, work on their audio quality.
- Enhance ambient sound: Press this button in addition to using earbuds to bring out the nuances of conversation.
- Modify sound: You can freely adjust the sound to suit each ear, which will improve

your listening pleasure.

- Silence all clamors: For security, weaken all alerts and sounds.
- Mono sound: Produce sound system variations in mono mode.
- Left/right sound equilibrium: To adjust the left/right balance for speakers connected to your device or another audio source, use the sliders.

Interaction and dexterity

Availability features can be set up while using your device to assist with adroitness problems.

Alternate Input

You come into contact with numerous data sources and controls in order to make use of your device.

○ Select 🧍 Accessibility > Cooperation and smoothness from the Settings menu. Next, select one of the related options:

- Multifunctional switch: Use your personalized adjustments to operate your device.
- Menu on the right: Make devices easier to use for people with limited dexterity.
- Voice Access: You can use a device without using your hands thanks to this feature. Open apps, tap buttons, type, open parchment, and much more with voice commands.

Interactions

It is possible to enhance the movements required to respond to calls, as well as to warnings and alerts.

○ Select 🧍 Accessibility> Association and ability from the Settings menu. Next, select one of the related options:

• Making and concluding calls:

- Say guest names aloud: Use Bluetooth or headphones (separately supplied) to hear the names of incoming calls read aloud.
- Respond subsequently: Respond to calls automatically using Bluetooth

or earbuds (which are separately accessible) after a predetermined amount of time.

- Press the Up key to answer calls. The Volume keys can be used to answer phone calls.

- Press the Side key to end calls: Press the Side key to end a call.

• For better collaboration control, redo the screen cooperation regions, hardkeys, and console.

Touch-sensitive settings.
You can adjust your screen so that it reacts less forcefully to contacts and taps.

○ Select 🧍 Accessibility > Collaboration and ability from the Settings menu, then select one of the related options:

• Contact and hold delay: For this method, choose a range of periods.

• Tap length: Calculate how far back a cooperation needs to go in order to be considered a tap.

• Ignore rehashed contacts: Establish a deadline for how long rehashed contacts are ignored.

Mouse and console

Set up the actual console and mouse that are connected.

o Select ⨁Accessibility > Collaboration and smoothness from the Settings menu, then select one of the accompanying:

• Pointer end to programmed activity: When the pointer approaches an article, it will instinctively tap on it.

• Tacky keys: By depressing each critical in turn, you can access console easy routes when you press a modifier key like Shift, Ctrl, or Alt. The important components that were still in place pushed down at that moment.

• Slow keys: Adjust the duration for which a key should be held in order to prevent accidental key presses from being interpreted as being squeezed.

• Skip keys: Determine how long to wait before allowing a key to be pressed again to help you avoid inadvertently pressing a button at least a few times.

Advanced configuration

Additional accessibility features and services can be customized for your device.

Concept: Additional open-source applications are available on the Google Play store.

Alternative methods of accessibility

Open the settings, select accessibility > High level options, and then select one of the options below:

    • Availability button: Select the Openness button's open alternate path.

    • Side and Volume up keys: Press and hold the Side and Volume up and Volume up buttons at the same time to quickly design some availability highlights to open.

    • Volume up and down keys: You can program an administration to start after three seconds of holding down and pressing the appropriate keys.

Notifications

○ Select ⊗ Accessibility > High level menu from the menu by opening it, and then select one of the options below:

• Streak notice: When you receive cautions or hear alerts, either the screen or the camera light will streak.

• Take Action Right Now: Determine how long alerts (such as warnings) that urge you to act quickly but are only displayed briefly should remain visible.

Installed apps

You can set up additional support services on your phone.

○ From the Settings menu, choose ⊗ Accessibility > Installed applications.

☀ Note: Anytime an additional availability administration is sent, it is noted and scheduled here.

About Accessibility

You can find information about the legal status and permit of the openness programming under Settings.

Select the option for Openness > About Accessibility from the Settings menu. The supplementary information is available:

• Rendition: Make use of the most recent programming variant available.

• Open-source licenses: Examine the specifics of the available open-source licenses.

Get in touch with us

If you have any additional comments about your device, please contact Samsung support via Samsung Individuals. Gain access to more resources, such as error reports, chat sheets, remote assistance, and much more (whenever supplied by your specialized company).

○ Select "Get in touch with us" under " Accessibility" from the Settings menu.

Other settings

Configure your smartphone with easier-to-use design options.

Concepts and the customer guidebook

Consult your device's user manual for some helpful hints and tricks.

○ Select the Tips and client handbook from the Settings menu.

Double-Messenger
Use two distinct records for a comparable use case.

1. Select Progressed highlights > Double Messenger from the Settings menu.

2. To empower the element for each supported application, tap the symbol of the application.

- Press Use a different contacts list to manage which contacts interact with the optional courier application.

-

Smart concepts

Depending on how you use your device, get suggestions for useful tasks like messaging and scheduling events.

- o To enable the component, select Advanced highlights > Wise ideas from the Settings menu. Then, press one of the options that appears.

Clinical data

Even if your phone is locked, crisis responders and other individuals can still access your clinical records.

1. Select Wellbeing and crises > Clinical data from the Settings menu.

2. Add a summary of your current medications, any sensitivity you may have, and any other clinical information you would want to have on hand in case of emergency.
3. Select "Save."

Labs

Analyze the analysis's key points. It is understandable that a few highlights won't function properly in every application.

1. Select Labs under Cutting edge highlights from the Settings menu.
2. To bring up a trial include, tap.

Concerning the phone

View details about your device, including its current configuration, legal nuances, programming and equipment versions, and much more.

1. Select About Phone from the Settings menu to view your phone number, model number, serial number, and IMEI details.

2. You can tap additional items to view more device information.

Idea: If you select ⓘ About phone > Status data, you can view the FCC ID of your device.

Samsung Knox

When it comes to Samsung devices that have undergone security testing with an eye toward large-scale enterprise use, the brand Samsung Knox is associated with the organization's security stage. It might be necessary to pay an additional permit fee.